Champions Again
The Story of Liverpool's 30-Year Wait for the Title

Ian Carroll

HAWKSMOOR
PUBLISHING

Published in 2020 by Hawksmoor Publishing.

ISBN: 978-1-8380990-7-7

Front Cover Image: Trent Alexander-Arnold mural painted by Akse; used with kind permission of The Anfield Wrap.

Front Cover Design: Richard Taylor.

Liverpool Football Club, Trent Alexander-Arnold, and other individuals listed in this book, are not associated with this publication in any manner.

To my newest cousin, Max Bernie-Ray Carroll.

Be proud that you're a Red.

CHAPTER ONE

Thirty years of hurt, frustration, and bewilderment, and three decades of failure in the top flight of English football, all came to an end on the 25th of June 2020. Liverpool, at last, were title-winning champions again.

The club ended the season with a massive haul of 99 points from 38 matches. It was the second-highest points tally in league history, just one behind the record. It could have been more, but for the inevitable 'taking-your-foot-off-the-gas' that occurred when Liverpool sealed the title with seven matches to spare. This, in itself, was a record.

Liverpool had won their opening game of the season, beating Norwich 4-1 at home. At the end of the first day of matches, the club lay third in the league table on goal difference.

By the time they completed their second match, a 2-1 away win at Southampton, Liverpool were top of the league. It was a position they would never relinquish on their relentless march to the coveted Premier League title.

They raced into an incredible early season lead over closest rivals Man City, and won their first eight matches to rack up maximum points. It looked like the club might go the whole campaign undefeated.

In game number nine, a draw against bitter rivals Man Utd saw Liverpool drop points for the first time in the season. This minor setback, however, spurred the team on to win their next 18 matches in the league. By the time their run eventually came to an end – with an uncharacteristic away defeat at Watford – the club had racked up 28 league games without loss, winning a magnificent 27 of those matches.

At that point, Liverpool were well on their way to becoming Champions of England. They could add this crown to the others they held at the same time, as Champions of Europe, and of the world. Not a bad treble to have.

At this point, all opposition had been crushed and nerves had been soothed by a spirit of optimism engendered by the club's manager, Jurgen Klopp. The players carried his philosophy and winning mentality onto the pitch. They simply refused to give up on their dream. They made it happen. They were, in Klopp's own words, 'mentality monsters'.

It seemed like nothing could stop them. Their quality was breathtaking. Their appetite for success insatiable. It was only a matter of time. In fact, we were talking a matter of a fortnight. Just a couple more weeks would have seen the team get over the finishing line, and win the much-coveted Premier League title.

And then, with the prize that the club and its fans most cherished so tantalisingly close, the football season was suspended due to the outbreak of Covid-19, the corona virus.

There was disbelief amongst the club's faithful followers. How could this be happening when we were within touching distance of the prize? It seemed like a cruel twist of fate.

No-one, not even Gary Neville or Alex Ferguson, could deny that Liverpool deserved to be Champions. But, would that actually happen? Would the season be cancelled? Would it go down in history as the season that ended prematurely, never really happened, and had no winner?

The possibility was too awful to even contemplate. The imminent sound of laughter was heard brewing 35 miles along the M62 and across Stanley Park.

We didn't want to be the moral victors. We wanted that trophy. Wanted it bad. Wanted it – in truth – with all our hearts. We had waited so long for this.

Too long.

Thirty years.

Once, we were kings. Then, we were cast out into the wilderness occupied by the also-rans.

What would have been considered madness three decades earlier, that the club's 1990 league title win would be our last for 30 years, had come to pass. That win was Liverpool's 18th league title in total. Our biggest rivals, Man Utd, had only managed seven up to that point, across their whole, so-called illustrious history.

By the time that Liverpool eventually became Champions again in 2020, to make it title number 19, United were sitting there smugly with an eye-watering tally of 20.

What had gone wrong? What on earth had happened?

How, despite picking up a grand total of 14 trophies in the interregnum, had Liverpool lost their grip on the league title itself, the competition that the club's legendary manager Bill Shankly had once called 'our bread and butter'.

This is the story of the accidents and incidents that occurred during that long hiatus. From Champions once to Champions again, and everything that happened in-between.

With managers (good and bad), and players (from the sublime to the ridiculous), as well as analysis of off-the-field events – including the changes of ownership – this is a time to reflect on WTF just happened before we hopefully sail off into another glorious period of prolonged success.

With fans still isolated and quarantined, and no immediate prospect of a well-deserved victory parade, let us reflect instead on the story of this great football club as it straddled those two great highs in 1990 and 2020.

Bookmarked by success at either end of this tale, there is much to examine, ponder, love, and regret, in those intermediate years.

There may also be some lessons to be learned along the way, so that we never have to spend such an interminable period out in the cold again.

During the painful era when we were languishing, and United were top-dogs, we still managed to occasionally bag ourselves a trophy and prove ourselves an irritant. But only occasionally; periodically.

We'd soon fade away again. Close, but no cigar.

I remember my dad saying, 'When we were great, they were shite'. That was in the 1970s and 1980s. He added, 'And when they were great, we were good'. So, on balance, we edged it.

But how had we lost our mojo? And how did we get it back? And what happened in all the years – the three decades – when we almost had it, nearly had it, or never even remotely came close to having it?

The answers are all here as we explore that incredible journey from 1990 to 2020, and the long and frustrating quest to become Champions Again!

CHAPTER TWO

In the 1960s, Liverpool were a club going places, muscling their way into the upper echelons of English football. Despite such lofty opposition as Leeds and Man Utd, the red-men of Anfield barged their way into the argument, and then simply refused to budge.

By the early to mid-70s, they were the dominant team in the land, and still had plenty of room for improvement.

And improve they did. Shankly resigned, but the legendary boot room continued. Bob Paisley took the helm, and he didn't do half-bad! Eventually, he'd rack up three European cup wins to top his domestic success.

When he lost Kevin Keegan to Hamburg F.C., he simply brought in Kenny Dalglish who, for a large majority of Liverpool fans, is simply the greatest player ever to wear the shirt.

I probably have my own personal favourite, as I was just a little too young to appreciate the player I was watching, even though I saw Kenny play many, many times. He does though, for his spells as club manager, his empathy and leadership at Hillsborough, and his playing career and continued championing of the club, stand as my all-time LFC hero. Long live King Kenny.

Bob Paisley once said, when asked if Kenny had been brought in as Keegan's replacement, that we would have kept them both. He added, with no small amount of wit and self-deprecation, 'I might have won something then!'

The late-70s and early 80s saw Liverpool crowned as both the best team in Europe as well as England.

The 80s were a decade of unparalleled success.

Though our neighbours across the park, Everton, rose to great heights themselves in the middle of that decade, we still edged them in two Cup finals and in our overall trophy haul. We had competition, but we always seemed to find another gear.

But there was tragedy, too.

Thirty-nine Juventus fans lost their lives at the Heysel arena in Belgium at the European Cup Final when supporters clashed in a crumbling stadium. English football teams were banned from European competition.

The Liverpool football manager, Joe Fagan, retired; a broken man in the aftermath.

Kenny Dalglish, one of the team's star players, was asked to take over the reins.

It was a move that shocked the fans of every club in the land, including our own. No-one saw it coming. No-one knew how it would work out.

We needn't have worried. In his first season in charge, Kenny won the League and FA Cup double; the first time in the club's history that this had ever been achieved.

In fact, it was only the second time that anyone had done the double in the history of English football. Not bad for a newbie.

Just to make sure that the team got over the finishing line, Dalglish also scored the winning goal in a 1-0 away win at Chelsea to seal the title. That's how you do it, he might have said!

Such was Dalglish's dedication to his new role that he started to leave himself on the bench so he could better concentrate on events taking place on the pitch. One journalist commented that Kenny Dalglish was the only manager in English football who wouldn't pick Kenny Dalglish!

I remember going to one game at Anfield, where we appeared to be cruising. I think we were 2-0 up with about ten minutes to go.

The Kop were singing Kenny's name and clamouring for his introduction. So on comes Kenny. The game's nearly over, right?

Well, all of a sudden, it all starts to go to pieces. Maybe the players felt they no longer had a manager on the sidelines judging them and calling the shots. The opposition rallied. I think they got a goal. The fans in the stands and on the Kop got extremely nervous. We wanted to see the king on the pitch, but not at the expense of losing the game.

We made it to the end of the game, victory intact, but it had been a scare.

I think it was the end of Kenny the player-manager. From now on, he'd be the gaffer, and that was that.

We lost another talisman in Ian Rush. Our leading scorer and the focal point of our attacking play. He left for Juventus.

To fill this sizeable gap, Dalglish brought in not one but three attacking players. It was a bold move. In fact, it was a stroke of genius.

Despite the success that the club had enjoyed in the previous decade and a half, Liverpool had never been ones to splash the cash. While Man Utd had forked out £1.5m for Brian Robson in 1981, Liverpool managed to win four European cups in eight years, as well as nine league titles between 1972 and 1986, and they had still not broken the million-pound barrier.

Their most expensive player was a defender, Mark Lawrenson, purchased from Brighton for £900,000 in 1981.

With the money that Liverpool received from Juventus for Rush, Dalglish splashed the cash.

He bought John Barnes, an exciting winger, from Watford; Peter Beardsley, a tricky centre-forward and playmaker; and John Aldridge, a lower-league goal-scoring machine and life-long Liverpool fan.

Then Liverpool's critics accused Dalglish of, well – cruelty – I suppose. How could he take the best team in the land and inject it with a totally new and devastating front-line?

Dalglish responded by saying the money from the sale of Ian Rush was no use to him sitting in a bank. The fact he'd managed to spend it on three terrific players was not his problem. It was, in effect, quite the reverse. The players were simply a joy to watch. They gelled from the opening match, and they became a supporters' dream for the next few seasons.

Our closest rivals, by this point, were Nottingham Forest. Champions of Europe twice in the previous ten years, the clubs would contest for both league and cup honours as the 80s drew to a close.

On the 13th of April, 1988, Forest came to Anfield, the bastion home of Liverpool F.C. The resultant fixture became known by many sports observers as the match of the century for the quality of Liverpool's play. They destroyed their opponents by five goals to nil.

Tom Finney, a legend of the English game, and by then an old man, was watching in the stands.

Bill Shankly once described Finney as the best player ever to grace a football field, and that the statement would still be true if the man was playing in his overcoat!

Finney spoke to commentators after the game and said it was the greatest game of football that he had ever witnessed. Sublime did not come close.

Liverpool won the league that year, and lost the FA Cup final to Wimbledon; denied another double.

The following year, they lost the league title in the last game of the season at home to Arsenal, but managed to win the FA Cup in an emotionally-charged final at Wembley.

And why the emotion, apart from the obvious intensity surrounding our nation's favourite sport?

One word: Hillsborough.

The truth of our downfall is this. Man Utd never knocked Liverpool off their perch. Sheffield Wednesday did.

Hillsborough was the beginning of the end for 30 years.

CHAPTER THREE

Hillsborough: the football ground that dare not speak its name.

In 1981, during an FA Cup semi-final between Tottenham Hotspur and Wolverhampton Wanderers, dozens of fans were injured in a crush at the Leppings Lane end of the ground. Thirty-eight supporters were treated in hospital, some with broken arms, legs, and ribs.

The resultant enquiry found that Sheffield Wednesday, custodians of the club, were guilty of selling too many tickets for that end of the ground. The recommendation and directive was to reduce the capacity.

For the next six years, the FA refused to hold semi-finals at the ground, allowing the club to make the necessary changes and put their house in order.

Then, in 1987, with the English Football Association looking for a stadium in the north to hold another semi-final, Hillsborough was mentioned as a possibility.

The conversation must have gone something like this.

'What about Sheffield Wednesday's ground?'

'Oh, we don't use them because of what happened in 1981. We told them to reduce the capacity in that end.'

'Well, they must have done it by now.'

'Yes, they must have done it by now.'

No-one asked. No-one checked. And no, they had not.

In 1988, Liverpool faced fierce rivals, Nottingham Forest, in the FA Cup semi-final at Hillsborough.

I was there. It was horrendous.

I was with a group of pals. We used to go to every home game at the time, as well as a number of away games. And this was something else.

My mate's brother was lifted up into the stand above the Leppings Lane terrace, as were many others, as the people looking down (with pity) upon us, sought to rescue us from what were clearly uncomfortable circumstances.

Me and my mate left the area behind the goal and moved to one of the side pens, seeking relief.

I remember standing next to one of my dad's closest friends, Tony Monroe. He'd been to more than 1,000 matches over the years. He'd been to most of the football grounds in the top tier of English football, as well as many across Europe.

Tony was about six foot three. He towered over most of the fans around him.

We were all wedged in, arms trapped by our sides.

Tony was screaming at the top of his voice, 'What the fuck is going on?!'

It just wasn't right, by any standards.

Twelve months later, we were back at the same ground, facing the same opponents. We had triumphed the previous year, and we hoped and somewhat expected, to do so again.

I walked up to the ground with my best pal, having travelled up in a convoy of five cars; four or five of us in each.

Some people had gone for a pint or had gone to the chippy before the game. We'd all do our own thing and reconvene after the game.

Me and my mate approached the ground at about ten to three, ten minutes before the scheduled kick-off time on a bright, clear, Saturday afternoon in April.

Unbeknown to us, there had been huge congestion at the turnstiles. The crush had been so bad that the Chief Inspector of police, in charge of affairs that match-day, had ordered the opening of a concertina gate to let the crowd in and avoid casualties.

It was a sensible move. Or so it seemed.

No thought was given to where the two or three thousand fans might go next, once access had been granted.

There was only one visible entrance into the arena from the concourse behind the gate. It was a tunnel that ran under the Leppings Lane stand and deposited spectators in the two pens right behind the goal.

Always a popular vantage point, the terraces behind the goal were already jam-packed. An extra two or three thousand people entering that area meant only one thing.

Disaster.

My mate and I presented our match tickets, coveted semi-final tickets no less, and entered the stadium.

Where should we go?

We headed through the tunnel, and into the already crowded – and then super-crowded – pens behind the goal.

We tried to find a vantage point.

We jostled and hustled our way further into the melee.

We caught each other's eyes. This is horrible. But still, we persisted. We were fans. There was always hustle and bustle involved in moving from one standing spot to another.

Then, we were suddenly thrown forward about 15 feet. We were spun around 180 degrees. It was like being sucked into a whirlpool. We had gone 15 feet forward in an instant, when there were no 15 feet to find.

When the maelstrom appeared to settle, we watched as people climbed up on to the railings in front, and attempt to haul victims and the suffering out of the crowd.

My mate recognised one lad who was pulling people out of the thick mass of supporters pressed up against the metal fence at the front of the terrace, there to keep the fans away from the pitch.

We knew something was wrong.

We moved into the next pen, the entrance to which was via the same tunnel. But trauma was in the air. We knew we weren't watching a football match anymore. That game was over.

Soon, so was ours.

Bruce Grobbelaar, the Liverpool goalkeeper, got wind of events off the pitch. He turned his back to the game to see what was happening.

The news travelled to the match officials.

The game was halted. The tragedy was not.

'Let's get out of here', said Hero.

That was my pal's name.

He'd rescued a family from a house fire when he was a kid; he'd had the nickname ever since.

We walked back up the tunnel, to make space for those to come.

They came.

At first, nothing seemed to happen for a minute or two. Had we over-reacted? Was this par for the course?

Then people started to emerge from the tunnel with one arm resting over the shoulder over a friend or fellow supporter.

After that came those who needed someone at either side of them to keep them upright.

Then came people being carried, as if borne on a stretcher.

And then came the dead.

In all, 96 Liverpool supporters lost their lives at Hillsborough. They were young and old, men and women, native Liverpudlians and people from all across the land. In other words, a wide variety of football fans.

Then came the funerals. Dalglish and all of the Liverpool players and staff did themselves great credit, and at no small expense to themselves. We felt we were at one, the club, the fans, the city (and credit to all of the fans of other clubs, especially Everton, who shared in our grief).

Eventually, life went on. Football resumed, though it did not feel the same. We won the FA Cup, lost the league, and tried to carry on. For the 96. May they never walk alone.

But it's not that easy, is it?

Grief takes time, needs time, and it cannot be ignored.

We rolled forward as a club towards the end of one decade and the beginning of another. Our team was still impervious. Our position was still number one. But it would be our last hurrah for a while.

CHAPTER FOUR

After dominating English football throughout the 80s, you'd have got fantastic odds on Liverpool going 30 years, from 1990, without winning another title.

The calculation would have dwarfed the 5,000 to 1 that the bookies offered on Leicester lifting the League trophy in 2016. You could probably add another zero to that.

Still, it happened.

After the pain of Hillsborough, there were still several matches to play in order to complete the 1988/89 season. Liverpool were granted a short period of grace – a little more than two weeks – when they played no matches. Results elsewhere meant that by the time the club resumed the season in early May, they were five points adrift of leaders Arsenal.

Liverpool's first game back in the league was an emotional match against local rivals Everton. It ended in a 0-0 draw.

I went to the match. It felt like a wake. The football felt unimportant. The pain felt all too real. I watched it, but couldn't really react to events on the pitch. I just felt numb.

Maybe in honour of the fans that had died, or maybe just because these guys were professional footballers, the players soon took up the mantle. The Reds won their next four league matches.

Sandwiched in-between games three and four in the series came the FA Cup final, to be played against Everton. We had come through a replayed semi-final against Forest, and now faced our neighbours for the second time in under three weeks.

At Wembley, supporters, myself included, were allowed to sit on the running track surrounding the ground. We wouldn't be hemmed in, and we were afforded the space to watch the game in a manner that felt appropriate. Sit in your seat, or sit on the running track. It's your choice.

The stewards just let us get on with it. It was like a 60s love-in. It felt right, and relaxed, and in keeping with the emotions tied up in the occasion.

And Liverpool won, beating the Toffees 3-1 to lift the cup.

Six days later, Liverpool faced Arsenal in the final match of the season. Liverpool held a three-point advantage. Arsenal had to win by two clear goals to take the title on goal difference.

The season had already gone on for long enough, due to the extension caused by the tragedy at Hillsborough. The game would be played on a Friday night. And then we could go home and put the season's events behind us.

With two minutes to go, the match was not going according to plan and the London club led by one goal to nil. That result would still see Liverpool crowned winners if they could just reach that tantalisingly-close finishing line.

In an iconic moment, the Reds captain, Steve McMahon, can be seen telling his team-mates there are only a couple of minutes to go, urging them on to one final push. See the game out, and Liverpool would be champions of England.

Then Michael Thomas of Arsenal ran through on goal and slipped the ball past the goalkeeper, Bruce Grobbelaar.

Cue delirium amongst the Highbury faithful in attendance, and utter disbelief and disappointment on the Kop, where I was stood.

The game had hardly kicked off again when the final whistle blew.

Arsenal were champions. Liverpool were runners-up.

My friends and I left almost immediately, off to the pub to drown our sorrows. Many Liverpool fans, to their credit, stayed and applauded the Arsenal players as they paraded the trophy around the ground.

At first, The Gunners had taken the trophy to their own fans. They thought the ground would have emptied around them, but the majority had stayed.

The Arsenal players thought they'd be hemmed in a corner with their own supporters, but they soon picked up on the mood that Liverpool fans wanted a chance to show their appreciation. They ended up doing a lap of honour.

I think the response that greeted Arsenal was an acknowledgement of a worthy opponent who had come out on top (though by the slightest of margins) over the long campaign that is the English football league. Overall, they had edged it. They were champs. We were not.

We hadn't fallen at the final hurdle; we had tripped up, two yards (or two minutes) from the finishing line. But, que sera, sera. Hopefully, we'd take our medicine and come out fighting for the following season.

And we did, sort of. We won our first match against Man City, and then followed this up with two draws; both earned away from home. By the end of August, we lay fifth in the table, but it was still very early days.

September began with an away win at Coventry, before a staggering 9-0 win at home to Crystal Palace.

I was living and working in London at the time, and as it was a midweek match, I couldn't go to the game. This was an era of few televised matches. I couldn't even get a commentary on the radio. Instead, I waited for the ten o'clock news when hopefully they would read out the football scores.

The newsreader read out the result and then added, 'Yes, you heard me right. Liverpool beat Crystal Palace by nine goals to nil!'

It seemed like the team that had crushed Forest by five goals in the game of the century had rediscovered their groove. Perhaps they had never lost it?

The next two matches involved a draw with Norwich and a victory over Everton at Goodison Park. How our city rivals must love us!

By the end of October, a victory over Spurs saw Liverpool go top of the league for the first time that season. Goal difference, for sure, would not be a problem this time around.

November saw a difficult return for the club to Hillsborough where, perhaps unsurprisingly, Liverpool failed to perform and suffered a 2-0 defeat.

By the end of the month, we were still top of the league, by count of goals scored, but we were level on points with Arsenal, Aston Villa, and Chelsea.

Come the end of the year, and the end of the 80s, Liverpool were four points clear at the top of the league after an impressive run of results in December.

Our most bitter rivals, Man Utd, were languishing in fifteenth place, just two points above the relegation zone, under manager Alex Ferguson.

The 1990s began with a draw against Forest, followed by an 8-0 trouncing of Swansea in the FA Cup third round.

The team continued to pick up points in the league, and remained consistent enough to either hold the lead in the title race outright, or share it with their nearest contenders; the ever-important goal difference constantly in The Reds favour.

Aston Villa and Arsenal were our rivals but, despite their close attention, Liverpool had another league and cup double in their sights.

We had been just one game away from achieving that feat in each of the two previous seasons. Could we do it this time?

That dream ended on the 8th of April when Liverpool lost the FA Cup semi-final to Crystal Palace, the same team they had thrashed so convincingly earlier that season. Alan Pardew, later to manage the

Eagles, put up a good old-fashioned, no-nonsense display to score the winner in extra time.

John Barnes had put The Reds 3-2 up with just two minutes left of normal time before Palace equalised and went on to win the match by four goals to three.

Though hopes of a double were ended, the league was still very much Liverpool's for the taking.

We finally sealed the title at the end of April with a 2-1 home victory against Queens Park Rangers.

My mates and I went to the pub to celebrate. It was a league title win, but hardly one that surprised us. We had won it six times in the previous ten years. We were always there or thereabouts. The feeling was one of happiness and satisfaction, but not elation, or euphoria. Not like now.

We won our last two matches to end the season with 79 points, nine clear of Aston Villa in second place. We had won 23, drawn ten, and lost just five of the 38 matches.

Our goal difference of 41 was more than twice that of anyone else. We had scored 78 goals all-told, an average greater than two per game.

John Barnes finished as our top scorer in the league, hitting the back of the onion-bag 22 times. Ian Rush and Peter Beardsley both got into double figures in a free-scoring team.

Dalglish, King Kenny, was our magnificent manager. He had been in charge for five seasons and had won three league titles in that time. And that as a newcomer to the management game.

It was league title number 18 for Liverpool. No one else even came close to those numbers. Everton and Arsenal were next best on nine, just half of our total.

The 80s had started for The Reds where the 70s had left off. Now the 90s looked like they were about to do the same.

Except sometimes things don't turn out quite as you expect, and the wheels would soon come off the Anfield juggernaut.

The end would be sudden and unexpected. We'd had the high of almost two decades of continued success; now comes the in-between bit, of what happened from 1990 to 2020.

In any good story, second act trauma makes for third act magic.

Here's ours.

CHAPTER FIVE

The champions rested, and the champions returned. The 1990/91 season began with a club-record eight straight wins at the start of a season, taking maximum points. They would remain unbeaten for the first 15 matches, dropping their first points in an away draw at Norwich at the end of October.

Highlights along the way included a 4-0 drubbing of Man Utd at Anfield, with a single goal from Johnny Barnes and a hat-trick from the little wizard Peter Beardsley. The first of the three was a tap-in. The second was a deftly-struck first-time shot from just inside the box. The last was a delightful lob over the United keeper after a quick free-kick from Ray Houghton. Sublime stuff.

It was our biggest victory over our most bitter opponents for 65 years. The newspapers were effusive.

The Guardian said, "This time it seems Liverpool are determined not to let potential rivals for their League title even dream a little."

Liverpool's first defeat came in December at Arsenal. This for a season that had kicked-off back in August. Things were looking good. Could the champs retain their title? By Christmas, it certainly looked that way. Before the match, Liverpool held a six-point lead at the top of the table over The Gunners. By the end of the match though, that lead had been cut to three.

The Reds then won four of their next five games, including a 3-1 win away at Tottenham, themselves unbeaten at that stage. Again, the papers had much to say.

The Times wrote, "LFC yesterday illustrated that they have not only the strongest squad in the Football league but also the finest tacticians. A line-up excluding Peter Beardsley and Ray Houghton, which provoked astonishment when it was announced at White Hart Lane, proved to be perfect for the occasion."

The only loss in that recent sequence of matches came via a 1-0 defeat away to Crystal Palace.

By the close of 1990, Beardsley had scored 11 goals in the league. Ian Rush had scored nine. Barnes had scored seven. The team had hit the back of the net 37 times in 19 matches; a rate of almost two goals per game.

Beardsley then sustained a knee injury and, in January 1991, Kenny Dalglish, the club manager, spent half a million pounds to bring in the combative David Speedie from Coventry.

Many pundits, as well as a few fans, questioned Kenny's judgement. Three goals in the centre-forward's first two games – one against Man Utd, and a double against Everton – showed that there was some wisdom in the call.

Speedie was 30-years-old when he joined Liverpool. Dalglish had reputedly wanted to sign him four years earlier when the striker was in his prime. Now, surely, he felt he could still do a job, and would provide cover for the injured Beardsley.

The fiery Scottish centre-forward managed more than 500 league games in his career so, despite starting his working life down the coal mines, he was certainly no mug. He finished with over 150 career goals.

Liverpool began the New Year with a 3-0 win over Leeds, before succumbing to three draws in their next three matches.

They ended this uninspiring run with a 3-1 victory against neighbours Everton.

Just over a week later, the same two sides met for a fifth-round tie in the FA Cup. The match was played at Anfield, and resulted in a 0-0 draw.

Three days later, on the 20th of February, 1991, the two teams met at Goodison Park for the replay.

I remember my uncle saying he didn't have a ticket for the match. I had one.

I was still quite ambivalent about football, its place in my life, the guilt that I felt going to the game when others had lost their lives doing that very same thing.

How could I cheer and pretend that what was happening on the pitch was everything, when I knew that life itself was more important?

I had been to Anfield for the league game just 11 days earlier. I had been back to our home ground for the first cup-tie, just 72 hours before the replay. Did I want to sit through it again, thumbing my nose at the dead, getting on with my life?

I didn't.

It would probably be another nil-nil anyway, and as much as I appreciated Everton's support through our Hillsborough days, I still hated playing against them. It's like fighting with family; we're all just too close. City rivals.

I gave my uncle the ticket. The game finished four-four!

Liverpool took the lead four times in the match, and each time, Everton equalised.

The last came with just moments to spare.

The next day, Kenny Dalglish handed in his resignation to the directors of LFC.

They asked him to reconsider. They couldn't quite believe what they were hearing.

'Take a sabbatical,' they advised, but Kenny knew he just wanted to go. He needed a clean break. Not a holiday. Not a few weeks off or a few months away, knowing he would have to come back. It had to end.

He'd come out in blotches. He'd been ill for a while. Since, well, Hillsborough. Attending every single funeral had taken its toll. Go figure.

Of course, he'd gone from being a player, to being a player-manager, and then to being the manager of the most successful football club in the land.

What he hadn't contended with was the 96 funerals he went to, and the support he, and the other Liverpool players, gave to all of the families of the deceased.

Add that to the career, the manager's position, the stress of maintaining the club's place as the best team in the country, and then you have, straw, camel, etc., etc.

Cue shock. Distress. Our talisman, probably the club's greatest-ever player, the manager who led us to our first domestic league and cup double, our hero, our king, was gone.

Kenny went on holiday. LFC went into meltdown.

While Ronnie Moran, a long-serving member of the Anfield boot-room was appointed as caretaker-manager, the club began to think about succession.

Moran's first game in charge ended in defeat, as they lost to perennial irritants Luton Town 3-1 on their infamous plastic pitch. They'd once failed to turn up for a cup match at Anfield, blaming icy conditions on the road. They failed to mention that their captain and talisman, Steve Foster, was injured.

I personally knew Liverpool fans who were working in London who returned home for that League Cup game. They managed to make it up the M1 and M6, but a professional football club somehow could not.

Dalglish was fuming. 'How could the opposition simply fail to turn up, giving about two hours notice that they were a no-show?' The groundsmen were all in attendance, the stewards, cleaners, and kiosk attendants were already there.

Don't worry, the Luton Town chairman offered in recompense. 'We'll pay for all the pies and hot-dogs that have gone to waste!'

I'm pretty sure Kenny had an idea where they could shove 'em.

But now Dalglish wasn't there. The job of maintaining Liverpool's lofty position fell to Ronnie.

After losing to The Hatters, Moran then lost an FA Cup tie with Everton, followed by a damaging home defeat against Arsenal, in what was still a two-horse title race.

It was a crushing blow to Liverpool's hopes of retaining the title. No one thought it would be our last for so many, many years, but it was slipping from our grasp.

The team and the interim-manager rallied to win their next three matches and returned to the top of the table, before two defeats and a draw in the next three matches effectively ended whatever hopes we had of scraping and scrapping to the end of the season.

Ronnie Moran was a Liverpool legend. He was a local lad who spent his entire career with the club, serving as captain and being an integral part of the title-winning team in 1964.

He became a coach at the club alongside Shankly and Paisley, Joe Fagan and Reuben Bennett. His association with the club had begun in 1952 and would last for almost 50 years. But he was still seen as a stop-gap in the top job.

In truth, the board felt like they were guardians of the goose that kept laying golden eggs, season after season. The trophies had kept coming for 25 years. They did not want the gravy-train to stop.

The media pressure was enormous, but it was all just noise.

'Who's replacing Kenny?'

'Is this the end of Liverpool Football Club?'

'When are you going to appoint a new manager?'

It's easy for me to sit here now and say what I know should have happened, and what I wish would have been done. I wasn't in the eye of that particular storm. I was just a heartbroken fan. I didn't have shareholders to answer to. I wasn't worried about a potential fallow period in our great club's history, and I wouldn't be held responsible for such an outcome as I wasn't a custodian.

But how I wish clear heads had prevailed. I would have loved it if the club had just left Ronnie in charge, or Roy Evans, another loyal servant, and had the club issue a statement along the lines of: 'Kenny Dalglish has resigned. Ronnie and/or Roy are in charge until the end of the season when the club will review its options and make a further announcement. Thank you and goodnight.'

And then kept schtum.

Let the press drive themselves crazy and write whatever they want. Stay cool, calm, and collected.

Instead, economics, and – no doubt – greed prevailed.

Who can we get in? Who will be just as good as Kenny, to ensure that we maintain the success that our fans and our shareholders expect?

There was only one man who fit the bill. His name was Graeme Souness.

CHAPTER SIX

One of the most controversial, combative, and also acclaimed midfielders of all-time is probably the best way to sum up the moustachioed one's playing career.

Souness signed for Liverpool in 1978 and went on to win three League titles, three European Cups, and four League Cups.

In 1984, he moved to Sampdoria in Italy, helping the club to the first Coppa Italia in their history in his first season there.

In 1986, he joined Rangers in Scotland as their first-ever player-manager. Following the success of his great friend and teammate, Kenny Dalglish, who occupied the same role at Anfield, it seemed like a successful working model.

In five years at Ibrox, Souness broke the Celtic stranglehold north of the border. He brought in established English football stars during a period when English clubs where still banned from playing in Europe following the Heysel stadium disaster.

During his short tenure, Souness won three Scottish league titles and three Scottish Cups. He was an abrasive figure. He brooked no quarter with either opposition players, opposing fans, or even the Scottish footballing body. He looked like he was ready to square up to anyone. And he often did!

He was close to the Rangers' board of directors. His feet were well and truly under the table. He could have stayed there for 20 years, possibly until retirement.

Then came the seismic shift at Anfield. Out of the blue, Dalglish resigned.

Liverpool panicked. They wanted to fill the void, and quickly. There was no 'let's see where the dust settles'. They had to make an appointment that would satisfy the media. They needed a name.

Graeme's was the one that fit the bill.

Club legend? Tick.

Successful manager? Tick.

Available? No bloody chance!

To be fair to him, Souness did not acquiesce easily to the approaches made. He did not come running at the drop of a hat.

'I'm alright here,' he seemed to be saying. 'Don't panic. Kenny will be back. He's my pal. I know him. Give him a few weeks and ask him again.'

But corporations wait for no-one. They pressured Graeme into it.

This club needs you, they said. There's no-one else who can fill Kenny's shoes except you. Rangers are good, but this is Liverpool. You have to help.

God, I wish Souness had picked up the phone to his old mate and got the low-down.

'You alright?'

'Yes. I am now. I've had a break.'

'Okay. I'm knocking the job back. Going to tell them to call you.'

'Thanks.'

That's all it would have taken! Thirty years of hurt would not have happened. Need not have happened.

Instead, Souness waivered under the Liverpool directors' entreaties. He gave up his cosy Scottish set-up and answered the call from LFC.

And it all went to shit after that.

Graeme took control for the last five games of the season. We were so close to completing the fixture list that a few weeks more would not have mattered under an interim-manager. Then, the club could have taken the closed season, a period of almost two months, to make a decision not born of the utmost haste.

To his credit, Graeme gave up so much to come and try and help. But 'try' is just about the most accurate description of his time in charge. We would soon be off the pace, and the changes that he instigated left the club bewildered and confused. We lost our compass. We lost our way. We fell off our perch. We became another has-been club.

You can't blame Souness entirely. When Dalglish took over as player-manager, that was a big shift, but at least Kenny was still there at the time. He knew the dressing room. He was a big part of it. He just changed his football shirt for a tracksuit or suit.

With Graeme, it was different. He'd left seven years earlier. His management experience was basically built one-on-one in the Glasgow rivalry with Celtic. He'd no recent experience of the English game, the exultant Arsenal, and the slowly emerging former giant that was Man Utd, not to mention the class act that was Leeds with the footballing aristocracy of Gordon Strachan, Gary McAllister, and their new signing Eric Cantona.

Souness was wrenched from his comfortable position at Rangers. He would have to hit the ground running, while learning the English league all over again, and at the same time making sure that Liverpool did not slip beyond pole position; that was what the world, the media, and the fans had come to accept.

Easy? You bet it ain't.

In his five matches in charge at the end of the 1990/91 season, Souness saw Liverpool win three and lose two of those games.

The League title went to Arsenal, winners by seven clear points with Liverpool runners-up.

A season that had started so positively had run out of steam. Effectively, the wheels fell off with Dalglish's departure.

Who would have thought that it would take so long to put things right? The twists and turns along the way are what this book is all about.

First of all, we have the Souness years. Could he do as a manager for the club what he had done as a player?

Sadly, the answer was to be no.

CHAPTER SEVEN

Melwood is situated in a middle-class suburb of Liverpool. It is the home of the football club's training ground. It is overlooked on all sides by modest semi-detached homes. It is, or was, just a collection of grass pitches, with barely a building of any note on the grounds. That is exactly how Bill Shankly had wanted it. And with good reason.

Shanks would have his players convene at Anfield each day ahead of their training session. The coach trip to Melwood would take 15 or 20 minutes. Then, it would be tracksuits off, and the training could begin, under the watchful eyes of the manager and his dedicated staff.

The system had worked well. Since Shankly was appointed in 1959, the club had enjoyed either intermittent or sustained success. There was clearly not a lot wrong with the facilities; however Spartan they appeared. The team practised for football matches there. Then they won the majority of those matches. Sounds good, doesn't it?

And there was at least some science or logic behind the system too. In Shankly's opinion, the last thing he wanted was showers or changing facilities at Melwood. You could probably ask any athlete, or even any normal person who goes to the gym, and they will tell you the same thing. At the end of any work-out, you're sweating. If you jump straight in the shower afterwards, you'll still be sweating when you get out. Object defeated.

Shanks thought that the 20-minute bus ride back to the stadium allowed the players to cool down again. Then, they could shower, get back into the clothes they'd left hanging on pegs in the dressing room, and go on their merry way.

When Graeme Souness arrived, one of the first things he did was upgrade the training ground. He wanted changing rooms, shower blocks, and all mod-cons. It was the first sign that a line had been drawn under all that had gone before. This was a new era. The Souness era.

You can't blame someone for wanting to stamp their own mark on things. Souness had his own vision, and part of that was the modernisation of facilities that may well have belonged to a different time. Still, it is a brave man who changes a winning formula, and a foolish one who changes it and then does not achieve at least the same level of results.

It was the same on the pitch. Too many changes happening far too quickly.

Out went Peter Beardsley to local rivals Everton. When we had first signed him, for an English transfer-fee record of £1.9 million from Newcastle United in 1987, he had managed just three league goals by the time we played the Toffees on the 1st of November. I remember the Blues fans taunting him with that old chestnut, 'What a waste of money.'

Quasi put a stop to that with a 70th-minute goal as we beat the Bitters 2-0. When he moved across Stanley Park to join the opposition, on his first return to Anfield, and still looking awesome, we serenaded back with 'What a waste of talent!'

As Souness prepared for his first full season in charge, he also dispensed with the services of able defender Gary Gillespie, journeyman David Speedie, and the promising young defender Steve Staunton.

He had lost the services of Alan Hansen, another seasoned-pro and Anfield stalwart, who had retired towards the end of the 1990/91 season after being plagued by injuries, and no-doubt feeling the loss of his great friend and fellow Scotsman Dalglish. Steve McMahon, Liverpool's inspirational captain for much of the club's successful late-Eighties period, would also leave mid-season.

In place of the departing players came Mark Wright, an England defender and a reliable lad, as well as striker Dean Saunders for another English League transfer record of £2.9 million.

Saunders was never a Liverpool player, not in a million years. I once watched a profile of Des Walker, the classy Notts Forest central defender. He'd been called up for England. Football Focus was talking about him and showing various clips of him in action.

They showed him marking Dean Saunders. But the clips did not so much show how gifted Walker was, but how bad Saunders was. He had no first touch. He couldn't control the ball. I think the correct expression is that he couldn't trap a bag of wet cement!

Any ball played into Saunders' feet would bounce two yards off him. All Des Walker had to do was nip into the gap between Saunders and the ball and either clear it upfield or pass it to a teammate.

Jan Molby, a classy midfielder for the Reds who spent 12 years with the club from 1984 to 1996, once said that, with no offence intended, when Ian Rush made runs in front of him, the prolific striker always knew how to stand off the opposition defenders so that you could always play the ball into him, preferably to feet or in front of him. It also meant that Molby had an outlet, which is vital on the football field when players from the other team are closing you down quickly and snapping at your heels.

With Saunders, Molby said you just couldn't find him. He'd run, but to what purpose? He was keen, and effective in front of goal for sheer effort and exuberance, and you couldn't fault his desire or commitment, but where was the guile? Where was the quality? He wasn't in Liverpool's league or class.

Though Saunders is a first-rate guy by all accounts, he managed just ten goals in the league that season, and he was moved on after a single year at Anfield, with the club recovering most, if not all, of their significant outlay on the player.

Souness also installed new-boy Mark Wright as club captain. It was another sign that the times-were-a-changing. As Wright himself later explained, 'That was Graeme though. He wanted to do so well and he changed so much, so quickly. I was aware that you should step up through the ranks, but here I was immediately made captain.

'Legends like Whelan, Rush, Molby, and Nicol had been at the club for ages and, with hindsight, me being made captain upset a few of them. It caused problems with those old-school players.

'Souness cared so much. He was a winner, but I think he maybe lacked a bit of patience, and it just turned out to be the wrong move.'

The result was a schism between the old players and the new, which is never a good thing. Two camps into one team just doesn't go.

That season's league campaign kicked off, and Liverpool were hit-and-miss. They won one, lost one, drew one. Won three on the bounce, then drew, lost, and then drew the next three. It was hardly title-winning form.

They then won, lost, drew, and drew again.

Won, drew, won, lost.

The calendar year ended with three straight draws against Man City, Queens Park Rangers, and Everton.

These things take time. We had a new manager who was trying to stamp his mark on the team and the club.

Players can take time to adapt. So can managers.

But where was this new project headed? Could it sustain the success that the fans had become used to? Could it improve on it? At least live up to it?

The New Year seemed to offer new hope.

January was seamless. Four straight victories in the league. Back on track.

We were still facing an uphill struggle to overhaul the leaders at the top of the table, but it was still early in the season. We're only halfway through. Stranger things have happened.

And then came the February blues. Defeat at home to Chelsea, a draw away at Coventry (I think I was there), a crushing 3-0 loss away at Norwich (Norwich!), and a nil-nil draw at home to Southampton on the 29th of the month. It may have been a Leap Year, but I can't imagine there was too much leaping going on, either on the pitch or on the Kop.

March was a mixed bag. Five games saw Liverpool win one, lose one, win one, lose one, win one. The team was proving to be a Jekyll and Hyde proposition. Maybe it was still half Dalglish's team, half Souness's.

April began with a miserable home loss to Wimbledon. That FA Cup final win, a few years earlier, had certainly given The Dons belief.

Liverpool then lost away to Villa, drew 0-0 at home with Leeds, and were trounced by four goals to nil at Arsenal with two goals by the effervescent Ian Wright.

I remember watching him at a game at Anfield where we absolutely battered them. We were winning one-nil. Then Arsenal punted a hopeful ball upfield. It was a lost cause, but guess who chased it like his life depended on it? Yes. Wrighty.

He closed down our keeper, forced him into committing a foul in the box, and won and converted the penalty in a game that ended 1-1. You gotta give him credit.

We then drew with Forest before beating Man Utd 2-0 at Anfield for a false-dawn, end-of-season high.

The last match of an uninspiring campaign ended with a blank draw against Sheffield Wednesday at Hillsborough.

Leeds won the league under their old-school manager Howard Wilkinson. Alex Ferguson was breathing down his neck, sensing his opportunity and that his time was about to come.

Liverpool finished sixth, their lowest league finish since 1965, a disappointing 18 points behind the eventual winners.

Between 1982 and 1991, the club had finished either first or second every season, winning the championship six times.

From 1973 to 1980, the club had done the same, number one or number two.

In 19 consecutive seasons, they had only once – in 1981 – failed to finish in either of the top two places. As compensation, they did win the League Cup and the European Cup that year.

It was the club's centenary year. Founded in 1892, 100 years later they were, or had been, a force to be reckoned with.

Now they were sixth. Sixth!

Consolation came in the form of the FA Cup. Victory in the final, with a man-of-the-match performance by new wunderkind and local lad Steve McManaman, at least put a smile on our faces.

It's funny that an FA Cup win should feel so unsatisfying. Maybe we Liverpool fans were just spoilt? Of course we were, but that doesn't mean that we wanted it to end.

The league was what really mattered, and we were well off the pace.

No-one could foresee just how bad things were going to get. That sixth-placed finish was a sign of things to come. The writing was already on the wall.

CHAPTER EIGHT

The 1992/1993 season represented the inaugural incarnation of the Premier League. With the introduction of satellite broadcasting, and the demand for more and more content in people's homes and in the pubs, the top tier of English football decided to break away from the league's own governing body and to side instead with the FA.

They would maintain the system of promotion and relegation between the lower divisions that were still operated by the football league, but this bit of distance between the two would allow the biggest football clubs in the land to snaffle an even bigger share of the pot of money made available by the likes of Sky and BSB.

From that attractive stream of revenue, the big clubs would now make 'solidarity payments' to the lower league clubs.

It was a whole new set-up. Same ball-game, just a lot more expensive.

This vastly-improved source of revenue would not be used to improve infrastructure or to lower ticket prices for the loyal fans who turned up week in and week out, generation after generation. Instead, it would be used to inflate transfer fees for players, and to line those same footballers' pockets with riches beyond their wildest dreams.

Can you kick a ball, stand up to a tackle and a bit of verbal, and perform in front of a crowd? If so, you're made for life!

Football was about to turn over a new leaf. No longer the preserve of the working class, it was now entertainment for the masses, including the wealthy and the middle-classes. Our future king, Prince William, is a Villa fan. Our Prime Minister at the time, John Major, supported Chelsea.

Liverpool were the holders of the FA Cup, but they were lagging behind in the league. Could they seize the opportunity presented by this new, dazzling landscape?

As in any close season, there are changes to be made. Players come, and players go. Some are moved on as being surplus to requirements, or they've failed to perform, or maybe they have reached the end of their contract and wish to explore pastures new.

Replacements are brought in to both fill the void, and to hopefully improve the first team or the squad as a whole.

This year, it would be Ray Houghton, Barry Venison, and the recently-purchased Dean Saunders who would be making way.

In their place came David James as goalkeeper, Torben Piechnik, and Stig Inge Bjornebye. Also joining this trio was Paul Stewart from Tottenham for a fee of £2.3 million. You could say that he was our marquee-signing that summer, but for me, he was a big flop.

Stewart has overcome a great deal of adversity in his life, and all credit to him for that. He had some great spells as a player and is not to be knocked, but I really think we paid over the odds for a player who just wasn't right for us.

When he was at Man City, the club chairman, Peter Swales, said that he wouldn't sell Paul Stewart, after a great season in the old second division, for £2 million. I think this was gamesmanship on Swales' part. He was probably planting the figure in the ether for someone to take a bite at.

Tottenham offered £1.7 million, and City accepted, despite what they'd said earlier.

I can remember Swales being interviewed with glee as he rubbed his hands at the amount he'd received for the player. He seemed to be saying, Spurs have been suckered.

So what did Liverpool do? They gave Spurs their money back and a whole lot more on top.

I'm no great reader of the game. I love football, and I think I know a good player when I see one, but I sometimes sit in the pub after the match, and if I'm with my dad and his mates and they're discussing the game, I sometimes think I must have been at a different ground.

'We're playing too deep.'

'There's no-one running in the channels.'

'So-and-so has got no pace.'

'We've got no width; it's all through the middle.'

I'm like 'Did we win?'

Funnily enough, my dad once took my sister to her first-ever football match. I must have been busy doing something else at the time, either working away from home or preoccupied with my music. (I sang with a punk band for two years, and bright spiky hair ain't a good look at the match!). Instead of dad and lad, it was then dad and daughter.

My sister gets home after watching her first game, and my mum asked how it went.

'Great,' my sister replied. 'We won three-nil.'

'No, we didn't,' said my dad. 'We won one-nil.'

'But you jumped up three times!' our Jacqui replied.

Anyway, I remember watching Paul Stewart play for Liverpool under Graeme Souness. He wasn't even joining in the game. It was happening ten yards in front of him.

Now I know that we have such a thing as a holding-midfielder, and that this became Stewart's game when he moved back from the forward line into midfield, but this was something else entirely.

It was as if the manager had said to him, forget about the game, son, you just rugby-tackle anyone who tries to break through. That's what Souness bought him for. To be a bully. To forget about playing football. To not join in the game-plan. We would try and win with ten men, and if the other team tried to do something about it, well we've got a stopper on the pitch called Paul Stewart and he'll have something to say about that.

Even with my limited footballing nous, I knew that this couldn't be right. And certainly not at £2.3 million.

In total, Paul Stewart spent three seasons at Liverpool. Originally purchased to play in the front line, his return from three seasons was precisely three goals.

Still, at least he wasn't overshadowed by Souness's other purchases that season, none of whom set the world on fire.

The truth is, Liverpool were off the pace before the season had even begun. They needed to make up a lot of ground, and the squad and recruitments made weren't good enough to take us forward. We'd barely manage to hold our own.

The traditional season opener was the Charity Shield, to be played at Wembley. It was a so-called friendly, played between the previous year's winners of the League and the FA Cup.

Some players, managers, and fans considered it a trophy in itself, and the previous meeting between the same two sides in this match, in 1974, ended up with two players, Kevin Keegan and Billy Bremner, being sent off for fighting.

Friendly or not, the game heralded the start of a new league campaign.

And Liverpool lost by four goals to three, courtesy of a hat-trick by the maverick Frenchman Eric Cantona.

It was a bad omen.

Just three months later, Cantona would join Man Utd and prove to be the final piece of the puzzle in Alex Ferguson's blossoming side.

Cantona was an enigma. A feisty, fiery, firebrand of a man and a footballer. He'd once suffered a bit of a hammering in a match by three opposition players.

After the match, he waited for them in the car-park, and when they emerged, took on all three at once. And won.

He was six foot three and a bear of a man, but boy could he play.

He'd arrived at Leeds just the season before, winning the league in his first campaign on English soil.

But he was away from home, and must have been missing his wife, for he soon struck up a friendship with the wife of a teammate. She was an actress. Cantona was a poet in an athlete's body. With a Gallic accent. The pair hit it off. Then the husband found out and hit the wife. Then the shit hit the fan.

Alex Ferguson was round at his chairman, Martin Edward's, house one Sunday. Leslie Silver, his counterpart at Leeds United happened to phone while Fergie was there.

As they were chatting business, Alex realised who Edwards was talking to and scribbled on a piece of paper, 'Ask him about Eric Cantona'.

Clearly, the off-the-field action was causing ructions in the dressing room.

For just over a million quid, Leeds agreed to sell their troublesome star.

Many managers might have shied away from a player who seemed to court controversy. He'd once thrown a ball at a referee who had booked him, turning his yellow to red and exacerbating the problem. At the subsequent disciplinary hearing, where Cantona was banned for a month by the Board, he reacted by approaching the bench and calling each of the adjudicators an idiot. The ban was doubled on the spot.

At this point, the Frenchman announced his retirement from the game. He was 25 years of age. Gerard Houllier, and the French footballing legend Laurent Blanc, as well as a psychiatrist, all tried to talk him out of it. Why not try England? They might have been quoting Shakespeare in Hamlet. 'There, no-one will notice you are mad!'

In 1991, six months into Souness's reign at Anfield, he had been told that Cantona was available. Liverpool had just beaten Auxerre in the UEFA Cup second round, the club where Eric began his career.

Aware of Cantona's reputation, Souness declined. He was trying to build a team, not throw a firework into the dressing room.

Elsewhere, Alex Ferguson was intrigued. He was quite friendly with Gerard Houllier (of whom so much more later), and had asked him about Eric.

'What's he like? Is he any good? Is he nuts?' that sort of thing.

Houllier knew everyone involved in and everything about French football. He had prepped the national youth teams, had coached the up-and-coming generation as well as the established talent, and played a huge part in that whole era that would soon see France crowned as champions of Europe and of the world.

He was the conductor for that whole passage of play. As such, he knew all of the French players, and his role brought him into contact with many of the world's great footballing men and women: chairmen, directors, managers, and administrators.

When Fergie posed the question, several years before signing Eric, it was borne out of pure curiosity.

'Great player,' said Gerard.

Cantona's impact was there for all to see.

The astute Ferguson, with a working-class Scottish eye for value for money, plus a desire to keep the recalcitrant one motivated, offered Cantona a contract of five grand a week basic wages, a five grand bonus for every game that the team won, plus a further five grand for each goal that the Frenchman scored.

Canny or what? It certainly did the trick.

Ferguson, Cantona, and United would soon reap the rewards that Liverpool had thrown to the wind.

CHAPTER NINE

Liverpool began the 1992/93 League season with a 1-0 defeat away at Notts Forest. They then came from behind to win 2-1 against Sheffield United in their first home game of the campaign. The attendance barely scraped over the 33,000 mark, roughly 10,000 less than the ground's capacity.

The club's lowly sixth-placed finish the season before was hardly setting pulses racing amongst the fans.

A home defeat to Arsenal was then followed in quick succession by three uninspiring draws against Ipswich, Leeds, and Southampton. The Reds put an end to that dismal run with a home victory against Chelsea, the match-winner coming courtesy of Jamie Redknapp, who had arrived under Kenny Dalglish as a promising 16-year-old from Bournemouth.

The attendance was again disappointing, not even managing to break 30,000. This for a match against Chelsea, played on a Saturday afternoon.

The next three games all ended in defeat for Liverpool. The opposition were Sheffield United, Aston Villa, and Wimbledon. These were matches we were usually expected to win.

We then beat Sheffield Wednesday at Anfield, before a testing trip to Old Trafford.

Two-nil up at half-time, Liverpool were dreaming of an unlikely away victory before two late goals from Mark Hughes – one in the 90th minute – earned United a draw.

Then came a win against Norwich, a loss away at Spurs, before we managed to string three straight wins together against Middlesbrough, Queens Park Rangers, and Crystal Palace.

This was hardly the stuff of dreams.

We lost to Everton, beat Blackburn Rovers, and were then crushed 5-1 away at Coventry. Things were just getting embarrassing now. This was not the Liverpool way or the Liverpool we thought we knew.

The calendar year ended with a 1-1 draw at home to Man City. What would 1993 bring?

Dissension amongst the ranks, for sure. Disappointment in the stands. A club without direction. It was not a happy camp, for the players or for the supporters.

We began the New Year with the same old problems. A home defeat to Aston Villa. Fortress Anfield had turned into sand-castle Anfield.

We then lost away at Wimbledon before winning 1-0 away at Arsenal, courtesy of a John Barnes penalty. Confusing or what. Where was the consistency? How could we win away at The Gunners and yet have lost at home to Villa three weeks earlier? Most depressing of all was our league position as we languished in 12th place, which was closer to the bottom than the top.

Then came two scoreless draws, against Notts Forest and Chelsea, before an away trip to Southampton on the 13th of February.

I have family living on the South coast. My birthday is in February. As a treat, I headed to the game with my dad and his mate Bobby, and we stayed with my aunt and uncle just up the road in Bournemouth.

We went to the match, and lost by two goals to one, with the late winner for The Saints coming via the aptly named 'Banger!'

That night, as we were stopping over, I went out for a few drinks. I bumped into a couple of old mates and ended up in a club. At the end of the night, I emerged onto the street with a young lady on my arm.

She spotted a friend. Her friend was climbing into the back of a car with one of the Liverpool players. This was one of my idols, and he was right there in front of me.

Apparently, Jamie Redknapp's old man, Harry, owned a wine-bar in the resort. The Liverpool team had all ended up there.

We approached the car. The girl I was with started chatting to her mate, while I took the opportunity to ask the player (who shall remain nameless) what had gone on earlier that day.

'What are we doing losing to the likes of them?' I asked.

His response shocked (but did not surprise) me.

'We'll be all right when we get shut of Souness,' he said, and then added, 'He's a wanker!'

The car door closed, the vehicle drove off, and I eventually returned to my aunt and uncle's home in the early hours of the morning.

We had a long drive ahead of us. My dad and Bobby wanted to set off early.

They were in the kitchen, tucking into a breakfast prepared by my aunt.

Rubbing my eyes after about two hours kip, I wandered into the dining room where everyone was sat.

I told them my extraordinary tale.

'I came out of a club last night with some girl, and she saw her mate, and her mate was with so-and-so. I went up to him and asked him what we were doing losing to Southampton, and he said "We'll be all right when we get shut of Souness. He's a wanker."'

'And then you woke up,' said my dad's mate Bobby.

And it did sound just like a dream, except it really and truly happened.

This was no bit-part player that we're talking about. This was a club legend, one of the biggest names on the team-sheet.

If *he* had no respect for the manager, what did that say about the rest of the players?

To be fair to Souness, he'd had serious health issues with his heart. Even three blocked arteries and a triple heart bypass couldn't keep him out of the game. He would later become an ambassador for the British Heart Foundation. If he considered himself well enough to continue in the Anfield hot seat, then all the fans wanted was for him to get us back to winning ways.

On the pitch, however, things did not look too good.

Two more draws followed before a home defeat to Man Utd which sent our fierce rivals top of the league and left Liverpool in 15th position, just three points above the relegation zone.

After a dismal February, where The Reds had played five matches in the league without a win, managing to score a miserly two goals in the process, the response to the disappointing Man Utd result was a much-needed three straight victories.

Liverpool edged past QPR, Middlesbrough, and Everton, winning each by a single goal margin.

Then came a draw and another defeat. We were now into April.

Traditionally, this is when the club would be honing in on another title. Now, nothing could be further from the truth.

Three wins and a draw from our next four matches ensured a top-half of the table finish, but it was all just so uninspiring.

Two more defeats followed, to Norwich and Oldham Athletic. Then came a resounding 6-2 victory over Tottenham in the last game of the season, with a double apiece from Rush and Barnes.

It was hardly cause for celebration. Man Utd finished as champions, their first title win for 26 years.

Liverpool finished a lowly sixth for the second season running.

This time, there would be no cup win as consolation. We had exited the League Cup at the fourth round stage. In the FA Cup, we had been knocked out in the third round back in January by second-division Bolton Wanderers.

In Europe, we had failed to make it past the second round of the Cup Winners Cup.

There would be no European football at Anfield the following season. In fact, would there be anything that you could even call football at all?

Would Graeme Souness fare any better in his third full season in charge?

For sure, it felt as if he couldn't fare much worse.

CHAPTER TEN

The pressure was mounting on Souness before Liverpool had even kicked a ball in the new season. His two full seasons in charge had brought two sixth-placed finishes.

The fans and the players weren't happy. Graeme Souness, a proud man with a winning mentality, could not have been too happy either. But he needed results.

Out went several squad players, including David Burrows, who I personally rated a lot. A Dalglish purchase, the defender had played 146 times for The Reds. I used to say, if you only threw one team-shirt into the changing room before a match, he'd be the one to come out wearing it. He gave it his all.

In came Nigel Clough, son of the legendary manager Brian, as well as Neil Ruddock, an imposing centre-half. One month later, Julian Dicks joined us from West Ham.

I was on holiday at the time. A group of us from Uni had gone to Tenerife for a late summer break before the next academic year commenced.

We were playing Everton. I went to the pub to watch it, and was confused to hear Dicks' name mentioned. Had The Toffees signed him? Had we?

I might have known. Souness had bought another bruiser, in line with his vision of the game. We lost the match two-nil.

The season had started with three straight wins (woo-hoo) before we were brought back down to earth when we lost 2-1 at home to Tottenham, the magnificent footballer Teddy Sheringham grabbing both of Spurs' goals.

When I say that I don't read the game of football so well, but that I think I know a good player when I see one, Sheringham was exactly that for me.

I remember watching him playing for Spurs at Anfield, when the ball was flying around our penalty box like a pinball. I was thinking 'please don't let it fall to Teddy'. My concern, the fact that I had my heart in my mouth, made me realise that I was watching one hell of a player.

Sheringham would later be offered to Liverpool. The board apparently decided that he was too old at 29 years of age. He went to Man Utd instead and won three League titles, the FA Cup, and the Champions League, scoring in both cup finals.

He continued to play professional football for a further ten years after his rejection as being 'too old' by LFC. He is definitely one that got away; the fact that he went on to strengthen our greatest rivals only adds salt to the wound.

Liverpool then returned to winning ways in the Prem. For one game.

They then lost to Coventry, Blackburn Rovers (under manager Kenny Dalglish), Everton, and Chelsea.

The Reds slipped from second to thirteenth in the league after those four consecutive defeats.

They then drew, won, and drew again, before beating Southampton at home in a match notable for a hat-trick from teenage striking-sensation Robbie Fowler.

The team had some exciting young talent about it in Fowler, Steve McManaman, and Jamie Redknapp, but they were still miles off being at the races.

October brought two wins and two draws. November brought two wins and one defeat. December brought one win and four draws.

Liverpool ended 1993 in eighth place, already a massive 20 points behind the season's eventual winners, Man Utd.

1994 began with an away win at Ipswich. Three days later, Liverpool took on their rivals from Old Trafford in a game at Anfield. It proved to be a cracker.

Bruce Grobbelaar, who would later be accused in a scandalous national paper of taking bribes to throw matches, conceded three times in the opening 24 minutes.

As bad as we were at the time, to be losing 3-0 at home in less than half an hour was simply unconscionable. I was at the match. Could it get any worse?

In the light of the accusations against our goalie, who had been with us through thick and thin and who had given us so many highlights, I still have to say that the jury is out.

Would he have sold us down the river to our most bitter rivals? I'd like to think not. Could he have saved any of those three goals? Well, he's close to a couple of them, hand outstretched. Could he have stretched a little further? Who knows.

Then Nigel Clough scored a minute later to pull one back, a 25-yard daisy-cutter that crept inside the post.

He then got another.

Finally, we got a corner. The box was packed. The ball was floated in.

Putting his head in where it hurt was Neil 'Razor' Ruddock. He came through a mass of bodies and powered it into the back of the net with his forehead, taking a decent whack for his troubles.

The game ended three-all.

Humiliation avoided.

For now.

In the FA Cup, Liverpool were again drawn against second division opposition. We had come unstuck the season before against Bolton. Now we were up against Bristol Rovers in another tricky third-round tie.

A draw away at Ashton Gate saw The Reds bring The Rovers back to Anfield, where surely we would triumph on home turf.

We lost 1-0.

Three days later, Graeme Souness resigned as the manager of Liverpool football club. The team had won the two League fixtures in between the Man Utd game and the FA Cup tie, but it wasn't enough to save the boss's job.

In his place came Roy Evans, moving from the boot-room to the hot-seat.

Evans was an amiable man. He was a local lad, a former England schoolboy international who played most of his football for The Reds as a defender in the reserves.

He began his coaching career at the club under Bill Shankly, and continued in the same vein under successive managers Bob Paisley, Joe Fagan, and Kenny Dalglish.

Souness was the fifth Liverpool manager he had served under, proving himself to be a loyal subject before he was finally given the top job.

It was a difficult time to take over. Not only were we well off the pace in the league, but the team were struggling for harmony and direction. Our competitors were streets ahead, and the demands of the game had changed as well.

With the succession to the Premier League format, and the vast swathes of money now circulating amongst the clubs, media scrutiny grew tenfold.

These well-paid players were now public property. The overseas interest in our national sport brought increased demand for a more exciting style of football.

Evans would have to learn fast.

On his first morning in charge, Roy parked his car in the Anfield car park and walked towards the staff entrance, where a horde of TV cameramen and journalists were gathered to snap their first glimpse of Evans in his role as manager of one of the world's greatest football teams.

Evans seemed surprised and bemused by the attention. He was unprepared for this level of interest. He must have been expecting business as usual, another day at the office, just with enhanced responsibilities. That was naïve on his part.

He greeted the waiting media with a genteel 'Good morning'.

Was this the man who was about to lock horns with Alex Ferguson up the road at Old Trafford and wrest the League title back into Liverpool's grasp?

It looked like he might go as far as to politely ask for it back, but there didn't seem much chance of him getting into a scrap.

After Souness tendered his resignation on the 28th of January, Evans' first game in charge was an uninspiring 2-2 draw with Norwich. We then lost away to Southampton and Leeds.

Then came a narrow home win against Coventry, followed by a 2-0 away defeat to Dalglish's flying Blackburn Rovers side.

Two home wins followed, against Everton and Chelsea, but then came two defeats against Arsenal and Man Utd, the latter chasing their second successive title.

Another defeat followed, at home to Sheffield United.

We then drew one, won one, and lost one, before winning away to West Ham.

There were two more matches to play in the 1993/94 season. We lost them both. One was at home to Norwich, and the other was away to Aston Villa. Both Villa goals came from Dwight Yorke in front of the Holte End, the last goals ever to be scored in front of that famous terrace before it was demolished at the end of the season to make way for a new stand.

Liverpool finished in eighth position on 60 points. We were 32 points behind eventual champions Man Utd. Kenny Dalglish's Blackburn, despite only being promoted to the Premier League the previous season, finished in second.

We were a long way away from being the club that we once were.

It would also be a long way back.

CHAPTER ELEVEN

In the summer of 1994, Roy Evans brought in a couple of defenders, for hefty fees, as he prepared for his first full season in charge as the manager of Liverpool Football Club.

He got off to a flyer with a 6-1 demolition of newly-promoted Crystal Palace. In the next match, Robbie Fowler scored a hat-trick in five first-half minutes as we beat Arsenal 3-0 at Anfield.

A 2-0 victory away at Southampton completed an electrifying August for the rampant Reds.

But it was not to last.

September saw the team draw with West Ham and Newcastle and lose to Man Utd, who were by now well and truly gloating after their two recent League title wins. Their near three-decade wait to be crowned champions was now over. Our own lengthy wait was just getting under way.

We then won our next two matches before losing 3-2 away at Blackburn Rovers, where Kenny Dalglish had hopes of going one better than his team's previous season's second-place finish.

Liverpool then won two, lost one. Then won two, and lost one again.

Then came four draws in quick succession.

Over the Christmas period and into the New Year, Liverpool won four on the bounce. Five, ten, or even 15 years earlier, this would not have been unusual. Now, it seemed like a near-miracle or a huge cause for celebration.

A home defeat against Ipswich in our next match soon put paid to such thoughts.

We won one, lost one, won one, lost one in our next four League games. We just could not shake the inconsistency.

Three draws were then followed by two wins before a 3-2 home defeat to Coventry.

We picked ourselves up to record a 2-0 win over Man Utd, who were locked in a two-horse race with Blackburn for the title.

The second of our two goals against United came with an 85th-minute own goal courtesy of Steve Bruce. How the Kop must have cheered at that one.

Alex Ferguson would later cite Steve McManaman's performance in the match as the reason United failed to win the league that season. Peter

Schmeichel once said that Fergie was obsessed with Macca. Every United teamtalk ahead of this fixture centred on how they could stop Liverpool's mercurial winger. This was high-praise indeed, but no more than the young lad deserved.

After we had temporarily halted United, we recorded four wins, two draws, and four defeats in our next ten matches before a fascinating last match of the season between Liverpool and King Kenny's Rovers.

Blackburn needed to win to be crowned Champions. If they failed to win, and Man Utd were to win their match away at West Ham, Ferguson's men would have collected their third title in a row.

I was at the match.

I know there were many people (mostly those of an Old Trafford persuasion) who expected Liverpool to throw the match. How could anyone expect our fans to want us to win and, in all likelihood, hand the title to the Red Devils?

Well, that just shows what you know.

We played, and we won, and we cheered when we did so, because Liverpool had won the match, and we are Liverpool supporters first and foremost, (and only Man Utd haters second).

And when news came in that Man Utd could only draw with West Ham, with record signing Andy Cole spurning chance after chance, well then we cheered even louder.

But we played it fair. And Blackburn Rovers won the league. Under Kenny Dalglish.

And how we wished that was us.

On a brighter note, we did win the League Cup that year, courtesy of another man-of-the-match display from young Steve McManaman, who was turning into the player that we all hoped he would become. He was a tricky winger, who was as capable of running as fast with the ball at his feet as he could without it. A rare feat indeed. He looked gangly, awkward, and lightweight, but boy could he play.

He scored two goals to help us lift the trophy as we beat Bolton Wanderers in the final at Wembley.

In the league itself, we had finished fourth. Better than eighth, and we had halved the distance between first place and ourselves from the previous season. It was progress of sorts, but still not the lofty heights that the club aspired to and that we still believed we could attain.

Our city rivals Everton inflicted further damage on Man Utd by beating them 1-0 in the FA Cup final. United were without their talisman Eric Cantona, who was out with a lengthy ban after hurling himself into the crowd to attack a Crystal Palace fan. He had just been sent off in a game for kicking out at Palace defender Richard Shaw. Then, an opposition supporter left his seat and approached the hoardings that separated the pitch and the stand.

After telling Cantona what he thought of him, the fan then found himself on the receiving end of a 'kung-fu' kick before trading punches with the three-time League winner and French footballing international. Not an everyday occurrence this, he probably thought, between taking a few well-directed smacks in the gob.

Cantona's employers sought to swerve outside sanctions by banning the player for the remainder of the season and fining him £10,000 (roughly one week's pay and a team win or a goal!). The FA, custodians of the Premier League, might have agreed to this had the Frenchman not confounded his critics in the press conference where he was expected to apologise profusely and instead astounded (and confused) everyone with his statement about trawlers, seagulls, and fish.

The FA increased the ban to eight months and doubled the fine. Eric's poetry had obviously fallen on deaf ears.

Another absentee from the FA Cup final against The Toffees was Andy Cole, a £7 million mid-season purchase by Ferguson that robbed Newcastle of their leading goalscorer, and the winner of the previous year's Golden Boot.

That Alex Ferguson's not soft. 'Newcastle look unstoppable. A real serious threat to our emerging hegemony,' he must have thought. 'I know, I'll just buy their best player. Make a ridiculous offer. They'll never resist a cheque with this many noughts on it.'

And he was right. But, as well as missing two clear-cut chances from inside the box in that fateful last game of the season at West Ham, either of which, had they gone in, would have won United their third League title in a row, Cole was injured for the final. The day belonged to Everton, and, despite doing the Double the year before, Man Utd ended the season empty-handed.

As for The Reds, Robbie Fowler was our top scorer with 25 league goals in 42 games. You might think that would have been enough to secure him the Golden Boot; however Alan Shearer at Blackburn scored 34 goals on their way to the title. Still, having only just turned 20 years of age, the Toxteth Terror had plenty of time on his side.

With another closed season under his belt, what changes would Roy Evans look to make? How many of the old guard would he keep, ahead of the emerging talent, and who would he bring in to help us bridge the gap? And, the million-dollar question. When would Liverpool climb back on their perch?

CHAPTER TWELVE

Roy Evans started his second full season in charge showing serious intent. Backed in the transfer market by his board of directors, no doubt recognising the ground to be made up, he off-loaded Nigel Clough for £1.5 million, let Ian Rush and Paul Stewart leave for free, and purchased, at great cost, Stan Collymore and Jason McAteer.

Collymore came from Notts Forest for an English record fee of £8.5 million, with McAteer costing roughly half that same fee. In all, a net spend of £11.5 million.

As a result, there was a spirit of optimism in the air. Would this be the season were Liverpool got back in the mix?

Arch-rivals Man Utd were still the ones to beat, while Blackburn were the current champions. Newcastle United, managed by another old Anfield favourite, Kevin Keegan, were looking to do what Rovers had done and rise from second division obscurity to the top of the Premier League in record time.

Only time would tell.

The season began with a 1-0 home victory over Sheffield Wednesday. The goalscorer was our new striker and record signing Stan Collymore, instantly endearing himself to the Liverpool fans.

We were then brought back down to earth when we lost away to Leeds United in a game played on a Monday night. With the riches presented by the satellite broadcasters came the requirement to serve up product on the most bizarre of occasions. As often as possible.

We're insatiable, seemed to be the diktat from the new paymasters. What next: Da, da, da, da, daaaa – the midnight match!

The Leeds game was settled by an absolute worldy from Tony Yeboah. A goal worthy of winning any game. It was a right-footed volley from outside the box that flew into the top corner, from a player brimming with confidence after scoring a half-volley with his other foot just a few days before against West Ham. If it's horses for courses with... errr... horses, then confidence is key for footballers.

It was time to pick ourselves up and go again. It was still early days.

We then beat Tottenham away. Barnes scored three. Unfortunately, the last was an own goal by the veteran striker in the 88th minute. Fowler scored the other goal for The Reds.

We then beat QPR 1-0 at Anfield via a Razor Ruddock goal, and then lost to Wimbledon away courtesy of an own goal from Phil Babb in a match that saw Vinny Jones sent off inside the first half-hour. With an hour still left to play, we failed to claw our way back into the game.

We then won our next two matches before we faced an away trip to Man Utd. The game ended in a draw, and was memorable for two goals from Robbie Fowler. The second of the two was an impudent dink from the edge of the box that pole-axed their keeper Peter Schmeichel.

Liverpool lad Steve McManaman, who set up the goal, ran up to his Scouse team-mate to celebrate and said, and I quote, 'You are fucking deadly!'

It was also Eric Cantona's first game back for Man Utd after his ban. He set up United's first goal, and then later scored a penalty to leave the match evenly-tied.

We drew next with Coventry, then beat Southampton away. In midweek, we played Man City in the League Cup.

City were not the team that they are now. No millions or billions bedecked their team or stadium. In Manchester at the time, certainly in the climate of the re-instated United at the top of the tree, Man City were their hillbilly cousins. Any team who failed to perform at Old Trafford would be greeted with a chorus from the stands of 'Are you City in disguise?!'

We beat the blue half of Manchester 4-0.

Years later, I was watching one of those traffic cop shows on TV. It showed CCTV footage of a car being side-swiped by a stolen car, which then sped off.

Policemen arrived and approached the damaged vehicle and the dazed but luckily unhurt occupants.

They were asked where they were going, and where they had been. They explained that they were on their way home from the Liverpool-Man City match when they were savagely struck, only barely escaping without serious injury.

The perpetrators had scarpered. Injustice all around.

'And how did the match go?' one of the coppers asked. We lost four-nil, came the reply. Injustice exacerbated.

Three days later, we beat the same team in the League 6-0 to add insult to injury.

We then lost four and drew two of our next six matches, one of which was to Keegan's Newcastle, who were by then threatening to run away with the league.

Eric Cantona, despite a decent first outing against us in his first game back, was showing the effects of his eight-month ban. He looked leggy, could no longer carry the team, and United were sluggish, allowing The Magpies to steal a march.

We helped to pile on the pressure with a 2-0 victory over Man Utd at Anfield courtesy of another Fowler double, as he continued to score goals at will.

By Christmas, Newcastle were ten points clear of the Red Devils. Fergie couldn't just buy their main striker this time. He'd have to keep something else up his sleeve. And boy did he!

A 2-0 win for Man Utd against their Geordie rivals on the 27th of December might have appeared a slight blow at the time, but would prove telling at the final reckoning.

Liverpool's own Christmas period saw a victory against Arsenal (with another Fowler hat-trick) and a draw away at Chelsea (with two goals from McManaman) to bring the calendar year to a close.

Cue 1996.

On New Year's Day, The Reds beat Notts Forest by four goals to two with another brace for Fowler and one for Stan Collymore. The two strikers were apparently not the best of friends, but a relationship was certainly developing on the pitch.

Despite his big money transfer, Collymore had refused to relocate, and instead made the long commute from his home-town of Cannock to training on Merseyside each day.

I remember our next-door neighbour once saying that he spotted a sign for the town while driving along the motorway, and decided to take a detour just to see what the fuss was all about!

Collymore would go on to play for England and have a decent career, but many felt he could have gone on to achieve much more in the game. He won just three international caps. While playing for Notts Forest, his team-mates would refuse to celebrate with him when he scored. Off-the-field incidents followed him throughout his career.

Fowler would later say in his autobiography that, rather than under-achieving, Collymore had actually over-achieved because people like him, (i.e., a little fragile up-top), were usually weeded out by the coaching system as they progressed through the ranks.

The rivalry could just have been professional, rather than personal, as the two strikers were at first vying for the single place available alongside Ian Rush in the Liverpool forward line-up.

The détente between the pair finally arrived during a game against The Gunners. Collymore set up all three Fowler goals, each of them put on a plate. Right there on the telly, it was possible to see dislike turn to admiration in front of your very eyes.

Liverpool then won six, drew three, and lost just one of their next ten games, before taking on title-contenders Newcastle United in a game voted the Premier League game of the decade.

By the 20th of January, The Magpies held a 12-point lead over Man Utd. They then purchased the Columbian forward Faustino Asprilla, one of the most talented and downright crazy players ever to grace this or any other league in the world.

I'd been watching him on some European football TV show for about three years. He never failed to catch my eye. I thought he was magnificent. A right-winger, he was simply unstoppable, a handful, unplayable.

In 1993, he was named by FIFA as the sixth-best player in the world, and this while appearing for lowly Parma in the Italian league.

When he joined Newcastle, I thought their success that year was assured.

And then they came to Anfield.

Fowler scored after two minutes to put us ahead, Collymore again doing the hard work, making something of an awful ball forward, then skipping past a defender, and setting up Fowler nicely.

Big Les Ferdinand equalised on ten minutes after some neat work from the crazy Columbian. Then Ginola scored four minutes later after skating past Jason McAteer who Roy Evans had converted from midfield to defence, for some unknown reason.

At half time, we were trailing by two goals to one.

In the second half, Fowler equalised after 55 minutes. Asprilla then put the Geordies back in front two minutes later with a beautiful shot off the outside of his right boot; the goal taken so quickly David James had no time to react.

Then came Collymore's intervention. He scored in the 68th minute to make it 3-3. That would have been a big enough dent in Keegan's ambitions, but the match still had more to offer in the way of drama.

This was a match that saw John Barnes pitted against Peter Beardsley. Kevin Keegan had emerged in a burgundy coat that would not have looked out of place on Top of the Pops. He later, wisely, put a Newcastle tracksuit top over it. But it did not spare his blushes.

In the 90th minute of a tense match, one that Newcastle needed to win to keep at bay the close attentions of Man Utd for the title, Collymore settled the tie after some deft footwork by John Barnes, crushing Geordie hearts and lifting spirits up in Manchester.

In the dug-out, Keegan slumped, as well he might. The game was played on the 3rd of April. Two weeks earlier, Man Utd had gone top of the table. Newcastle's lead had been whittled down after his infamous 'I'd love it if we beat them' rant, after Fergie suggested Keegan's team still had it all to do just a few games earlier.

The Red Devils had been on an incredible winning run since January. They'd won ten of their last 11 games, with five of those victories coming via a single goal by Cantona. Proof, if any were needed, of the Frenchman's value on the pitch.

The only draw in that sequence came away against QPR, which prompted Fergie's comments in the post-match TV interview, to which Keegan took such umbrage.

In the title run-in, Man Utd lost to Southampton and then won their final three league games.

Following defeat to Liverpool, Newcastle had won four, drawn two, and lost one of their last seven games.

It wasn't enough. Man United were champions. Newcastle finished four points behind them in second place.

Keegan should have read his Faust. Never make a pact with the devil.

As for ourselves, we won two, lost one, and drew three of our final fixtures following that celebrated, entertaining – but ultimately meaningless – game against the Geordies.

We finished in third place. This was better than the fourth place we managed the season before. We were closing the gap.

No longer 32 points behind the title-winning team, we were now just 11. Were they toying with us? If we'd got closer, would they have found another gear and simply accelerated away, or were we a team on the up?

We would soon have a chance to find out, as we had reached the FA Cup final, and we were about to play the League champions, our nemesis, Man Utd.

CHAPTER THIRTEEN

On the 11th of May, 1986, Liverpool travelled to Wembley to face Man Utd in the FA Cup final. I was there.

I travelled down to London with my mate Hero in the back of a nippy sports car that belonged to a bloke I occasionally worked for. He and his dad sat up front, and we sat in the back. We fairly flew down the M6 and M1 in record time.

We all had seats in different parts of the ground. It was difficult enough to get one ticket for a cup final, let alone a pair, so we all tried our best to remember where we had parked and arranged to meet up after the final whistle.

There was much-anticipation that we were about to witness a great game. The two teams were the top scorers in the cup that season, and the rivalry between us meant there would be no quarter given.

Man Utd had won three league titles in the previous four years. This was their third FA Cup final in a row, having beaten Chelsea two years earlier before losing to Everton a year later.

Crowned League Champions just six days earlier, United had little to lose. Their season was already successful. Ours was not. If they could win, they would complete a League and FA cup double.

We had to stop them. We would surely give it our all against our great rivals.

The teams came out for the traditional walk on the pitch, prior to kick-off, to soak up the atmosphere of this great occasion.

The players usually opt for a smart, dark suit, worn with a shirt and tie, and a pair of shoes.

Man Utd appeared in navy-blue attire, respectful and appropriate. The Liverpool team came out dressed in white Armani suits, white shoes, and brightly-coloured ties. This was certainly not combat-gear or battle-fatigues and suggested that the squad cared more about their appearance than they did about the trophy they were about to compete for.

How Alex Ferguson must have laughed. He must have been delighted. We had done his team-talk for him.

'Look at that lot,' he might have said. 'They think they've won already. They're straight off to the West End after the game to celebrate, in those self-same suits.'

How had this fashion faux-pas happened? No doubt, the fairly-relaxed regime under the fairly-relaxed manager was partly to blame. Surely he should have set the dress-code and, on having been informed of the players' intentions, curtailed them with a stern 'Not on my watch!'

Instead, Roy Evans treated the players as adults, as equals, almost. He cut them a lot of slack, at a time when there were many off-field distractions.

There was a spirit of optimism in the country. Cool-Britannia captured the zeitgeist of a nation as Blur and Oasis were battling it out at the top of the pop and rock charts and the Spice Girls were making history as the most successful all-girl band of all-time.

The young footballers of both Liverpool and Manchester United were mixing in the same circles as these pop-stars. Some of them were even sharing their beds!

They all had plenty of cash to throw around, and they were all basking in the celebrity spotlight.

Some of the footballers even acquired modelling contracts. David James, the Liverpool goalie, had just been signed up by Giorgio Armani.

James asked Armani if they'd like to design the team-suits for the cup final. How many of us wish that he hadn't.

The game itself was a close affair. Liverpool had plenty of flair, and more than a little steel. United could match us in both departments, but they could also better us with a recent track record of picking up trophies.

Dull it was. And tense. There was a lot at stake. For us, it meant an above-average season would be elevated that little bit further. It would also put a dent in our opponent's voracious appetite for silverware.

At half-time, the score was nil-nil. Roy Keane, in the Man Utd engine-room, was on his way to a match-winning performance as he sought to nullify everything Liverpool threw at them which, admittedly, did not amount to that much.

In the second half, it continued to be a closely-fought game. Where I was sitting, in the stand behind one of the goals, I sensed we were starting to get the upper hand.

Once or twice, Stan Collymore carried the ball forward (not literally) and put the United defence on the back foot, turning them inside out, almost teasing them as he started to ping in speculative crosses.

Surely, before too long, one of these searching balls into the box would be met by the predator Fowler?

Alex Ferguson must have felt the same way. In the 74th minute, he hauled off a striker, Andy Cole, and replaced him with midfielder Paul Scholes.

Fergie obviously felt the need to bolster his troops in the middle of the park. Even Roy Keane could not hold back the mounting tide of Liverpool attacks.

And then Roy Evans, on the Liverpool bench, did something unexpected. He hauled off Stan Collymore and replaced him with Ian Rush.

I'm sure this was a reaction to Ferguson's move, as it came just two minutes later. The United substitution was a response to our improved standing in the game. They had to do something as the game was turning against them.

The Liverpool substitution appeared to be tit-for-tat. We're drawing. They've made a change. We'll make a change.

It bore the hallmarks of an inexperienced manager. If only the manager had taken an alternative view, one borne of confidence. They've made a change because it's not going according to plan for them. That means we must have them worried. Let's keep doing what we're doing. We're fine as we are.

Instead, Collymore's shirt number went up on the subs-board. The player couldn't believe it. His look was one of complete shock. 'I'm killing them, here, boss' he seemed to be saying. 'Do you want to win this game or what?'

There can have been a no-more relieved person in the ground that day than Alex Ferguson at that moment.

Collymore was starting to run them ragged. They were struggling to contain him, hence the introduction of another midfielder to try to get close to him.

There was only one person that could have stopped Stan Collymore that day, and that was Roy Evans.

And he did.

It was now up to Rush and Fowler up front to try to latch onto some stray bit of play and snatch us a goal. Both of these players were goal-poachers. They needed someone to provide the creative spark. The rest of the team were duelling themselves to a stalemate against a strong United side. The one man who had license to try something different was now sitting in the dug-out.

With five minutes to go, United won a corner.

The ball came in, and David James punched it clear; except, it barely made it out of our penalty box. Instead, the ball landed at the feet of the last person you'd wanted it to, if you were a Liverpool fan.

Eric Cantona set himself up nicely with his first touch, and then unleashed a right-foot drive that made its way through a crowd of players with the accuracy of an Exocet missile before ending up in the back of the net.

There was hardly any time left in which to respond, and the game drained away to a United victory.

And as for the white suits? Well, as my dad says, they should have played in them. They wouldn't have got them dirty!

John Barnes later said that he was gutted with the choice of attire, too. As he was soon due to retire, he thought of all the use he might have got out of a dark Armani suit. It would have served him well for TV appearances, after-dinner speeches, and the like. Instead, it went into the wardrobe, never to be seen again.

As for The Reds, another season was now over. Another one with nothing to show for it. Still, another one would be along soon enough. There had at least been some progress made in the past 18 months. We'd risen from eighth place to third in the league, and had only narrowly lost out in the cup final.

We had some exciting young talent on our books, and those white suits would soon be forgotten, wouldn't they? (The answer is clearly 'no!')

So roll on 1996/97.

We were about to get New Labour. Would we get a new Liverpool, too?

CHAPTER FOURTEEN

A largely settled side, and a manager who had now been in the hot seat for two-and-a-half years, all pointed to the possibility that Liverpool could be serious title-challengers in the 1996/97 season.

Despite the common perception that the squad contained more playboys than players, we could still boast some of the most thrilling young talents in the country. If the first team were not quite delivering the results everyone wanted, the youth development side and the scouting system were certainly holding their own.

There was Robbie Fowler, Steve McManaman, and Jamie Redknapp. The three of them would have graced any club in the land. In the close season, Roy Evans purchased an exciting winger from the Czech Republic called Patrick Berger. He would go on to become a firm favourite amongst the fans for his wizardry; he was also quite popular amongst the female fans for his dashing good looks and his long flowing hair.

There were also two new names in the squad from the young side who had won the previous season's FA Youth Cup. Bootle-born Jamie Carragher and the free-scoring Michael Owen, one of the most sought-after talents in the land.

Owen was a prodigy. His father had played professionally for Crewe Alexandra and Everton, and Michael was destined to follow in his old man's footsteps.

He was selected for his area's under-11 team when aged just eight, and would go on to break the goalscoring record set previously by one Ian James Rush. Owen would manage 97 goals in a single season.

Aged 12, he signed schoolboy forms with Liverpool and continued his upward trajectory with a single-minded focus and an eye for goal that marked him out as a global superstar in the making.

At the age of 16, playing alongside team-mates who were in the main a couple of years older than himself, he netted a hat-trick against holders Man Utd in the quarter-final of the FA Youth Cup, before scoring five of Liverpool's seven goals in a two-legged semi against Crystal Palace.

He then grabbed an equaliser in the final against West Ham, a team featuring Rio Ferdinand and Frank Lampard, in a match where The Reds went on to win and lift the trophy for the first time in the club's history.

Promotion to the first-team squad then followed. To be honest, there was nowhere else left to put him. He had already shown himself to be the best player in the country at youth level, and even a spell in the under-23's would have been a waste of time.

Steve Heighway, who headed up the youth system at Anfield, thought him ready to make the step-up. Ready for anything, he went on to say. Anything that you can throw at him.

There was certainly a buzz about him. Rumours of greatness filtered through to the fans.

I was working in London at the time, restoring the Albert Memorial in Kensington Gardens. One of my colleagues was a Tottenham supporter. We'd regularly talk football.

He was a big admirer of Robbie Fowler, one of the most natural finishers the game has ever seen. Every Monday morning at work seemed to involve discussion of another Fowler goal, brace, or hat-trick, as he put it to the opposition week after week.

One time, my work-mate was effusing about how Robbie had done it again. I then told him about Michael Owen, the goalscoring records he'd already broken, and the excitement he was generating in the city amongst supporters of a red persuasion.

"They are calling him the new Robbie Fowler," I said.

'Hang on a minute,' he replied. 'The old one's only 21!'

Before the end of the season, we would all find out what the fuss was about.

For now, there was still a level of optimism that we could give it a real go this season.

For openers, there would be an away trip to Middlesbrough, who had just secured the services of maverick Italian forward Fabrizio Ravanelli. Nicknamed 'The White Feather' due to his prematurely grey hair, Ravanelli had won the Italian league, the European Cup, and the UEFA Cup with Juventus. His signing was something of a coup for The Boro.

That summer, England had played host to the Euro '96 football tournament. The country fell in love with the national game again. On the terraces, the sound of 'Football's coming home' rang out, as we willed Terry Venables' England team on to glory. Agonisingly, they would fall just short, losing to eventual winners Germany in a semi-final penalty shootout.

Anfield itself was chosen as a venue for three of the group games, and one quarter-final. Host cities were granted extended drinks licenses. Bars and clubs could stay open until six in the morning in an attempt to bring a little European culture to the sporting spectacle. It worked, and despite disappointment for the national team, the tournament was an overall success.

As a result of some superb individual and team displays at the Euros, there was an influx of foreign players into the English game. Chelsea snapped up Gianluca Vialli and Roberto Di Matteo from Italy and Frank Leboeuf from France. Man Utd brought in Karel Poborsky from the Czech Republic after their run to the final, where they eventually finished as runners-up, while we had signed our own import in Berger. Maybe the clubs and fans had never wanted the summer and the festival of sport to end. Many players had certainly put themselves in the shop-window, and English clubs came running in time for the start of the new season

On the 17th of August, 1996, Liverpool began their league campaign in the North East.

I was still living and working in London, but I had recently met a girl on a writing holiday in France. She was an Oxford-graduate, privately-educated, and lived in a large house in the hills outside of Bolton.

How did she fancy Middlesbrough, away?

Surprisingly, she said yes.

I got the train up from the capital the day before the game, and on match-day, the pair of us travelled up to Middlesbrough, again on the old choo-choo.

We booked a room for the night above a pub in the town, and made our way to the football ground.

It was a glorious summer's day. We were sat in the visiting-supporters section behind the goal. Full of new-season joy on the first day back, the Boro fans attempted a Mexican wave.

Around three sides of the ground, people raised their hands on cue and in celebration. When it reached the Liverpool end, the wave abruptly stopped. No-one joined in, and instead we regaled them with a chorus of 'What the effing hell was that!'

Luckily, my prim and proper lady-friend found it amusing.

And then we scored, through Stig Inge Bjornebye, not long after the kick-off.

Then Ravanelli equalised with a penalty after 26 minutes.

Johnny Barnes restored our advantage shortly afterwards, before The White Feather again restored parity to leave the half-time score at 2-2.

The Toxteth Terror then put us back in front halfway through the second half. We were dreaming of an opening-day victory before you-know-who – Ravanelli – popped up with another goal nine minutes from the end to grab a hat-trick and the headlines for himself, and a point for his new employers.

The game had finished three-all. I turned to my date and asked if she had enjoyed it. The match had certainly been entertaining. Had she seen enough goals, I asked.

'Well, I would have liked one more,' she said, and you couldn't really argue with that.

Still, a draw away from home wasn't a bad way to start the new campaign, and we would soon have the chance to improve on that as we were back in action just two days later with a Monday night game against Arsenal at Anfield. Liverpool emerged 2-0 winners thanks to a brace from McManaman, whose influence in the team was growing with each passing game.

A 0-0 draw followed at home to Sunderland before an away victory against Coventry, courtesy of a single goal coming, unexpectedly, from centre-back Phil Babb.

Collymore and that man McManaman again netted as we overcame Southampton, which we followed up with a 3-0 defeat of Leicester away, and a 5-1 demolition of Chelsea at home, with Patrick Berger (Paddy to the fans) scoring twice in each of those games.

A win away at West Ham at the end of September meant Liverpool were sitting comfortably at the top of the table, and supporters started to dream that our six-year drought might be coming to an end. Then up pop Man Utd to burst our bubble with a slim victory at Old Trafford.

Six wins, four draws, and two defeats in our next dozen matches saw The Reds end the calendar year with a five-point advantage at the top of the league table.

The highlight in that recent run of results was a 5-1 victory over Middlesbrough, where the prolific Fowler bagged four of the goals.

We were now looking down on the rest of the division. We were halfway there. But, football – as we know – is a game of two halves.

How would we fare in the following months?

Could the Spice Boys roll up the sleeves on their white suits?

If they could just back up their flair with a bit of grit and steel, the ability to grind out results, then we had put ourselves in a great position.

The green shoots of progress were well-and-truly visible. Would 1997 be our year?

CHAPTER FIFTEEN

The second half of the season began on New Year's Day, with a trip to Stamford Bridge to face Chelsea. Liverpool lost 1-0 to a goal by Di Matteo.

We then beat Burnley in an FA Cup game at Anfield to progress to the fourth round and a tie away at Chelsea, where we had a chance of some instant revenge.

We won three and drew two of our next five league matches. Collymore scored four goals in just three of those games. There was also a goal on his debut for the young midfielder, not yet a centre-back, Jamie Carragher.

In his entire Anfield career, which would eventually see Jamie notch up more than 500 appearances, he would score just a further two times. He also managed to score seven own goals, which meant he'd found his own net twice as often as he had that of the opposition!

On the 26th of January, Liverpool faced Chelsea at The Bridge. By half-time, we were 2-0 up courtesy of a goal each from strike-pair Fowler and Collymore.

I was at the match with four of my friends from Uni; three of them Chelsea supporters and the other one a Red.

How smug was I – and all of the Liverpool fans – as we surged to that two-goal advantage inside the first 21 minutes?

I remember commenting, as the Chelsea forward Gianluca Vialli was pinned back by his corner flag, that he wouldn't get many goals from there!

Chelsea were managed by Ruud Gullit, the brilliant Dutch midfielder who had recently taken the reins from Glenn Hoddle. Gullit would need to give a tactical masterclass to get Chelsea back into the game.

Warming up on the touchline, ahead of the half-time break, was Mark Hughes, formerly of Man Utd and a player loathed by Liverpool fans. He seemed to loath us equally in return.

A terrific centre-forward, it was felt that he was coming to the end of his career, and had been merely put out to pasture at Stamford Bridge. He was 33 years of age at this point. Surely his legs were giving out on him, and whatever pace he'd once possessed should have deserted him too.

As he ran past the Liverpool fans in the stand, and tried to limber up those ageing limbs, he was greeted by our own version of the former Man Utd chants of 'Hughsie', which was amended to 'Useless'.

So that's what we did. Serenaded him with a chorus of 'Useless'. And boy did it fire him up.

Not that he ever needed much encouragement to ram it down Liverpool's throats, but when he emerged as a second-half substitute, he proceeded to play like a man possessed.

Soon after coming on, with his back to goal, Hughes shrugged off the close attentions of our centre-backs to take a lofted ball on his chest, before turning and fizzing a low shot past David James in the Liverpool goal and into the net.

Shortly afterwards, Hughes threw himself at a loose ball at the edge of our box. To be honest, the ball could hardly be called 'loose'. By rights, it was in Liverpool's possession, but Hughes wanted it more, and he dived in as if his life depended on it, taking the ball out from under John Barnes's feet and turning it back into the path of Gianfranco Zola, who had joined Chelsea the previous November.

Zola, one of the modern greats, struck a 25-yard curling shot into the top corner to level the tie. Later in the game, two goals from Vialli completed the comeback and saw Chelsea run out eventual winners by a scoreline of four goals to two.

The London club would go on to lift the FA Cup that year, while Zola would win the Football Writers Best-Player award; the first Chelsea player to ever do so, and the only person ever to win it when not completing a full season in the English league.

A 1-0 defeat for Liverpool away to Aston Villa, was then followed by the visit to Anfield of Newcastle United.

Kevin Keegan had resigned suddenly in January 1997, to be replaced by none other than Kenny Dalglish.

The previous year's fixture had ended 4-3. Keegan's team were known for their attacking flair. Kenny was expected to take a more conservative approach.

No one was expecting a repeat of that earlier result, and the bookies were offering large odds on that score.

By half-time, Liverpool were three up courtesy of goals from McManaman, Berger, and Fowler.

With 20 minutes to go, The Reds held the same advantage, but the match was about to explode into life.

Three Newcastle goals in the next 17 minutes saw the scores levelled as the game entered injury time.

In the stands, Liverpool fans held their heads in their hands in despair, having seen the team throw away such a commanding lead.

One final attack saw Fowler drop deep and play the ball to Dominic Matteo, before making his way into the box. Matteo fed Bjornebye on the left wing, with the latter delivering a terrific cross which Fowler rose to meet, heading back across the Newcastle goalie Pavel Srnicek and into the net for another last-gasp Liverpool 4-3 victory. Geordie hearts were broken once more, and again in dramatic fashion.

In the dug-out, Stan Collymore was not as elated as he might have been with the team's victory. He had fallen out of favour with Roy Evans and had been left on the bench.

As he later admitted, he couldn't help but feel gutted that, the season before, it had been him scoring the late winner and grabbing the headlines. Now, he was down the pecking order and in danger of becoming a forgotten man; his Anfield adventure soon to be over, and his career never again to reach the same heights.

He would score just two more league goals for Liverpool, and was sold to Aston Villa as soon as the season ended. Despite a fee of £7 million, and the fact he was joining the club he had supported as a child, he managed just six goals in his debut season, and then just one in 19 games the season after that.

With less than two months of the season still to go, Liverpool and Man Utd were now neck-and-neck for the title. It was said to be a two-horse race. After a victory over Arsenal at Highbury, The Reds had seemingly relegated both The Gunners and Newcastle to fight it out for third and fourth place, while we could concentrate on a fight to the finish with our greatest rivals.

When United lost at home to Derby County, Liverpool had a chance to go top with just six games to go. A home defeat to Coventry meant we lost the opportunity; we remained in second place.

Man United still had to come to Anfield. A win in that match and we would be top with just three games of the season left to play.

We lost 3-1.

We then beat Tottenham by two goals to one to maintain a faint glimmer of hope, before defeat away to Wimbledon put paid to our dreams. The title was going to United. Again.

Still, a second-place finish would mean entry into the Champions League. No longer the preserve of just the title-holders from each

European country, the top two teams in England would now appear in the prestigious and profitable competition.

Going into the final match of the campaign, Liverpool held a two-point advantage over Arsenal and Newcastle.

Victory over Sheffield Wednesday would see The Reds competing against Europe's elite the following season.

We could only manage a draw.

Arsenal and Newcastle both won.

Kenny Dalglish's team took the runners-up spot.

Liverpool finished fourth in a two-horse race!

The only bright spot in a disappointing end to the season was the debut appearance of young Michael Owen. He got our only goal in the loss away to The Dons. His entry as a late substitute lifted an otherwise dire display where Owen's youthful exuberance and never-say-die attitude was in contrast to the dull performance of a team who appeared to have lost the stomach for the fight.

For many observers, Liverpool had been the best team in the land for much of the campaign. That they had failed to clinch the title was purely their own fault. They had thrown it away. Several of the players felt they should have won it.

Mark Wright, the Liverpool and England defender, said that we were better than Man Utd; better than everyone, in fact. Yet the team did not capitalise on that advantage.

Do you blame the players, or the manager, or both?

The next season would be Roy Evans' fourth in charge.

The Spice Boys name would linger, for as long as Liverpool continued to spurn the success that their fans desired and, indeed, the players' own talents deserved.

Would they use the hurt of this campaign to make a determined charge for the title in the 1997/98 season?

Despite the praise the team received for their style of play, and the promise of emerging talent like Owen, Evans could only point to one trophy, the League Cup win of 1995, during his tenure in the top job.

It was surely just a matter of time before Evans lost his position; unless he could find a way to get his team to win trophies.

CHAPTER SIXTEEN

Liverpool were struggling to shake off both the Spice Boys tag and the equally-damning verdict of 'nearly-men'. Where was the grit, the nous needed to turn draws into wins, and abject performances into well-earned points?

How were we going to derail the Old Trafford juggernaut that had cruised to the top of the English game?

We were in danger of being the baubles on someone else's Christmas tree. A team feted for its style and its conglomerate of youthful talent and exuberance but, ultimately, one that would be left to clear up the day-after debris of someone else's party.

For all the quality that we possessed, and the rich history that we had, it was all just a tad embarrassing.

We added Paul Ince, the self-styled 'Guv'nor' who had graced the Man Utd team as they finally shed their own cloak of underachievement and took their first steps on the road to success.

It was unusual for any activity to take place between the two great rivals: a situation that persists to this day. A two-year stint in Italy, with Inter Milan, provided the breathing space to allow the transfer to happen.

Roy Evans is a decent bloke. Sensitive too. He must have been acutely aware of what people were saying about the team, both in the media, and in the city itself. Scousers are sociable people. We like to communicate. No-one would have thought twice about telling Roy *what was what* if they bumped into him in the street, at the ground, or even at a wedding reception. He'd have been told what was needed, in no uncertain terms.

Steel was added. So too was experience, in the form of Karl-Heinz Riedle, the German striker who had netted two goals in the European Cup final for Borussia Dortmund just a couple of months earlier. Though he would be almost 32 years of age on joining The Reds, he was still clearly a force to be reckoned with, and no shrinking violet, as his brace against Juventus in the biggest club game in Europe had clearly shown.

Both of these additions were meant to bolster the squad, and also lend guidance and support to the youngster Michael Owen in what would prove his breakout season.

Though reports of his breathtaking talent were now common knowledge in the country, and despite scoring on his debut in the previous campaign, this would be his real opportunity with the first team. He would get chances. He would be expected to take them. Though still just 17 years of age, he would be in with the big boys.

We'd lost Collymore, but we had Riedle, and the emerging Owen. In midfield, we had Redknapp and McManaman, and now we had Ince, whose forceful presence should allow those boys to shine.

We'd had a couple of seasons where we were close, but no cigar. All of that bluster and false promise would be forgotten and forgiven if we could just gel and connect. We had to get ourselves across the line in first place and fulfil all of our undoubted promise.

Roy Evans had won just one competition after three-and-a-half years in charge. That was the League Cup, traditionally presented in February, when there were three months of the season still to go.

All of the big trophies: the League title, the FA Cup, and the Champions League, were all decided in May. By that time of year, we were usually planning our holidays with nothing left to play for, and that was as true for the players as it was for the fans.

As we prepared for the new season, we also said goodbye to club legend John Barnes. He moved to Newcastle on a free-transfer, thereby ending a decade at the club in which he had been simply magnificent.

My mum tells a story. She never goes to the match, but not long after my dad starting taking my sister to Anfield with him, my mother decided to join them to see what all the fuss was about.

They chose a Monday night game in May 1987. It was the second to last match of the season. Liverpool beat Watford by a goal to nil.

Afterwards, my dad asked mum what she thought of it.

'It was alright,' she said, not overly enthused. 'But I tell you what,' she added, 'we need to sign that winger from Watford!'

Five weeks later, we did. I think we should also sign me ma up as a scout.

Barnes played over 400 games for The Reds and scored more than 100 goals. Jamie Carragher – whose career at Anfield was just beginning as the veteran striker's was coming to a close – said, 'He's the best player I've ever trained or played with, great with both feet, and I'd say he's the best finisher I've ever played with, and that includes Fowler and Owen.' He added, 'Speak with the players from those great Liverpool sides and ask them who the best player they played with was, and they all say John Barnes.'

So it was farewell John, and thanks for the memories.

And what was Digger Barnes' favourite memory of his time at Anfield? As he told Leo Moynihan, in his book 'Match of my Life', is was that 5-0 victory over Forest in 1988.

Barnes said, 'That one night captured all that was great about our team. Movement, pace, flair, strength, it was all on show that season and 1987/88 is one that I recall fondly, a season where everything seemed to come off. I loved every minute of it.'

He effused about his teammate, Peter Beardsley, in the same memorable game.

'Peter was majorly in the mood,' said Digger. 'One scintillating dribble took him past four defenders with that characteristic shoulder drop of his and he smashed the ball against the bar bringing the Anfield crowd to their feet. Those fans had seen plenty of quality over the years and it took something special to get them up, but that night Peter had them out of their seats.'

Barnes concluded by saying 'It was a special night and a special team. I won't ever forget either.'

And nor will we. But life goes on.

Joining the club in the summer that Barnes left was a young midfielder called Danny Murphy – a Liverpool fan from boyhood. Proving that sometimes dreams really can come true, Murphy signed from Crewe Alexandra for a fee of £1.5 million. Now, instead of watching The Reds from the stands or The Kop, he'd be out on the pitch alongside his idols.

He would come to the fore in the following seasons but, for now, Murphy would have to bide his time. For sure, he was another promising youngsters; the club seemed to be bursting at the seams with them.

Could they turn this potential into silverware? Another campaign was about to start. With both Fowler and Owen up front, anything seemed possible, and with midfield general Paul Ince installed as captain, it was hoped that we could put the disappointment of the last few seasons behind us as we embarked on another league outing.

It would not be easy to overcome Man Utd or the growing menace of Arsenal under manager Arsene Wenger in his first full season in charge, but would the nearly-men finally get there?

It was time to find out.

Another addition to the squad was goalkeeper Brad Friedel, who joined from Columbus Crew in the USA for £1.7 million. He was brought in to provide both back-up and competition for the incumbent, David James, whose error-prone end to the previous season had cost Liverpool vital points in the title run-in, not least in the loss to United that effectively ensured our rivals would once more finish as champions.

We began the new campaign with an away draw at Wimbledon, with Michael Owen scoring our only goal from the penalty spot, resuming where he had left off the season before.

Our first home game resulted in a disappointing loss to Leicester City, before an away draw at Blackburn with Owen again on the scoresheet.

An away win at Leeds saw the first goal for Riedle, before four wins and a draw in our next five matches finally sparked our season into life. A hat-trick for Patrick Berger in a home win against Chelsea was a particular highlight in our recent run of good form.

Our bubble was then burst in the next match away to The Toffees at Goodison as we lost 2-0.

We quickly recovered to beat Derby and Tottenham, both by a scoreline of four goals to nil, before throwing it all away by losing at home to Barnsley.

Then came a trip to Arsenal, who were just getting to grips with a new regime and the new culture brought in by the visionary Wenger.

It's fair to say, when he arrived mid-season during the previous campaign, most Gunners supporters asked 'Who the hell is Arsene Wenger?'

It didn't help that his previous employers were Grampus Eight in the Japanese league.

Despite managing in France with Nancy and Monaco for ten years before Japan, and winning the league and the cup with the latter, he was still very much an unknown quantity to English fans.

All that would soon change, as Wenger stamped his mark on a team who, despite winning two titles in the past decade, were now firmly on the slide.

Wenger changed the culture of the club. There would be no more boozy nights out. No junk-food. No lads-on-tour mentality. He would turn these professional footballers into athletes. He monitored everything, from their pre-match meals to their alcohol consumption afterwards.

He managed to reassure the old-guard, including defensive stalwarts Tony Adams and Martin Keown, that they still had a future at the club. He also brought in fresh blood with the likes of Emmanuel Petit, Nicolas Anelka, and Patrick Vieira.

By combining the old with the new, and educating the whole group to his new world order, Wenger managed to close the gap on Man Utd, and stole a march on the whole country by taking football to a whole new level.

Indeed, Wenger quickly caught up and then got ahead of the game. Before anyone knew what he was doing, he had a fighting-fit unit with which to challenge the previous elite, which was beginning to look the preserve of one club: Man Utd.

The two teams would go head to head, and sometimes toe-to-toe, literally, in what would prove to be an entertaining few years full of on-field clashes between the pair.

We were about to find out if we had what it took to compete with Wenger's new Arsenal.

Thanks to a single goal, a sublime strike from Steve McManaman, we emerged one-nil victors at Highbury. From a seemingly-innocuous throw-in, the lad from Kirkdale let the ball drop over his shoulder and hit a right-foot half-volley from the left-hand corner of the box, the ball looping and dipping into the net. It gave David Seaman no chance, and was a strike that even Thierry Henry would have been proud of.

Could we consider this as a yard-stick for where we were? The next match was at home to The Red Devils. Beat them, and we could claim to be better than the two top teams in the land and, maybe, we could add some grit and consistency to the mix and finally make this season our own.

At Anfield, we lost 3-1. Optimism deflated. Again.

Still, Michael Owen was proving to be everything we had hoped he would be. Goals in his next three matches, all of which Liverpool won, showed that he could more than live up to the earlier hype.

We then won three and drew two of our next five matches. Even when we lost in the sixth game of that sequence, a 2-3 reverse at home to Southampton, Owen grabbed both of our goals.

In the next match, away to Sheffield Wednesday, in a 3-3 draw, the wonderkid bagged his first league hat-trick. It wasn't even his first treble for the club. That had come back in November in a fourth-round League Cup tie against Grimsby.

The whole country knew his name now. As well they should have. He had made his debut for the England team just three days earlier against Chile. In doing so, at the age of just 18 years and 59 days, he became the national side's youngest player of the 20th century.

A draw against Everton in our next fixture was followed by a trip to Aston Villa where, despite another goal from Owen, we lost 2-1 courtesy of a brace from their new signing, and our old striker, Stan Collymore.

We were now entering the month of March, with Man Utd having a seemingly-insurmountable lead at the top of the table. So much so that one bookie, Fred Done, actually paid out to punters on that basis. United held a nine-point lead over second-placed Arsenal, although the latter had two games in hand, and the two teams were set for a showdown at Old Trafford which would surely hand the title to United if they were to win.

Arsenal beat them 1-0.

In the aftermath of that defeat, Alex Ferguson attempted some of the mind-games that had worked so well against Kevin Keegan in that earlier title run-in, stating that The Gunners were bound to drop points in the matches to come.

They didn't. Arsenal went on a run of ten straight victories to finally seal the title against Everton with a 4-0 victory, the last of the goals a humdinger from their captain Tony Adams, who went marauding up the pitch and smashed the ball into the net with the nonchalance of a man playing footy in the back-garden against his five-year-old son.

It didn't even matter that The Gunners then lost their final two games of the season, including a 4-0 loss to Liverpool.

Arsenal were champions. United finished second. We came third.

It was to be another trophy-less season for The Reds. We were nearly-men again.

Michael Owen finished as our top goalscorer with 18 league goals. Other highlights were hard to find.

Ronnie Moran, Roy Evans' assistant, announced his retirement at the end of the campaign. He more than deserved the rest.

Moran had joined the club straight from school back in 1949. He had been playing football for Bootle Boys and knew a postman who delivered letters to the home of the then-Liverpool chairman.

The postie kept recommending Ronnie to him, and the schoolboy was eventually offered the forms to sign on as an amateur.

A week later, Moran was playing his last game for Bootle when he was told that a gentleman wanted to speak to him. The man said he was a scout for Everton and he wanted Ronnie to sign for The Blues.

'You're a week late,' Moran told him. It was their loss and our gain.

Ronnie Moran went on to hold every position at Anfield from player, to coach, to physio, to interim manager. A legendary member of the boot-room, he probably had more knowledge of the club than any man alive. A later biography about him was entitled 'Mr Liverpool'. After spending a total of 49 years with the club, he deserved that epitaph more than anyone else.

Who would come in to replace him? Who could accelerate this talented yet underachieving squad towards success?

We were about to find out, and the club was to take on a distinctly Gallic flavour.

Bonjour Gerard Houllier.

CHAPTER SEVENTEEN

Also with a Gallic flavour was that summer's World Cup, which was being held in France. This may seem like a diversion from the main theme of this book, but it had huge importance for our new star striker, Michael Owen, and what would happen during the remainder of his Anfield career.

England's opening group game was against Tunisia. An Alan Shearer goal in the first half saw England with a slender lead as the match moved towards full-time.

Owen was introduced as a substitute in the 85th minute. Just before the final whistle, England increased their advantage with a goal from Paul Scholes as we ran out 2-0 winners.

In the next match, against Romania, England were trailing by a goal to nil when Owen again came on as a substitute, this time in the 72nd minute. Nine minutes later, Owen equalised to set English hearts racing, before a last-minute goal by Dan Petrescu sealed the win for the Romanians.

For the final group game, a must-win match against Columbia, Owen was chosen in the starting line-up, partnering Shearer in attack.

England won 2-0 to set up their first knockout game of the tournament against the Argentinians.

The match would be remembered as both famous and infamous, and contained enough incident to fill the whole competition, never mind a single game.

First came a penalty for the Argies, when the duplicitous Diego Simeone skips past David Seaman in goal, sticks out a leg, and goes rolling over. Lucky to be given anything, he has the cheek to start waving an imaginary red-card in the air, urging the ref to take action and send Seaman off.

Batistuta then converted the spot-kick to give them the lead. There were six minutes gone.

Then Owen gets the ball and heads for the box. Now I always noticed this about Michael when he was playing for Liverpool. Give him the ball outside the penalty area, and his first thought – his almost single-minded ambition – is to get inside the 18-yard box at the earliest opportunity and in the most direct manner possible. I suppose that's where the action happens and, if someone is going to foul him there, well, it's a pen, innit!

So Owen uses his electric pace to go surging towards the Argentinian goal. As he attempts to skip past a defender, he is sent crashing to the ground. The result? A penalty for England.

I know I'm going to sound biased here, but please hear me out. After the game, and at certain times throughout his career, Michael was accused of going to ground a little too easily, and *this* incident was cited as a prime example. Really? What striker wouldn't? But, the 'evidence' drawn from this particular event is replays which clearly show the defender's foot and Michael's foot not meeting. And that's 100% correct. However, the contact takes place higher up. The defender has put his body across the oncoming striker. They clash at the knee, and that's what sends Owen flying.

Asked after the game if he'd conned the ref, as their defender seems to pull his foot out of the way instead of making the tackle, Owen replied – without recourse to the video replays or any of the punditry and debate in the studio – 'Well, it did make my knee bleed.' Obvious contact.

Penalty awarded. Shearer converted.

There were only ten minutes gone, and the game was already a classic.

And then everything stopped. And by that, I mean the world.

There were more than 26 million people watching on TV in England alone. That was more than half of the entire population. Numbers around the globe stretched into hundreds of millions.

Six minutes after England equalised, Owen found himself asking for the ball on the half-way line. David Beckham plays it into his path.

Owen drags the ball forward with the outside of his right foot and sets off towards the Argentinian back-line with two midfielders breathing down his neck and snapping at his heels.

To no avail.

Everyone at home, in the pubs, and in the stands is watching open-mouthed.

Michael is still running, and boy is he fast!

He's approaching the edge of the penalty box. He's bobbing and weaving, with no one really sure which way he's going to go.

Then, he shimmies as if to go left, and knocks the ball to the right with the outside of that right foot again.

In a flash, he's past the last defender, as the goalkeeper comes out to close the space and narrow the angle for a shot.

This is almost uncharted territory for any player, let alone an 18-year-old in his first international tournament, to find himself one-on-one with the goalie having raced alone through the entire Argentinian half of the pitch.

Luckily, Paul Scholes, an excellent player, experienced international, twice a league title winner, and five years older, was on hand to take on the responsibility of finishing off the move.

Scholes was perfectly positioned. The ball was running across his body, straight into his path. He had the whole goal to aim at, whereas Owen would need to swivel his torso and strike the ball back across his body with sight of only a fraction of the goal.

You can imagine the shout from Scholesy:

"Mine."

And the response from Michael Owen:

'Not bloody likely!'

The result was one of the finest goals in World Cup history, or football history itself for that matter.

The game itself ended in a 2-2 draw after Beckham's sending off, after another incident involving the spiky Simeone.

Knowing no other way to stop a superior England team, the South Americans targeted Beckham for a bit of 'argy-bargy'. When Beckham naively responded and got a red card, the game swung away from us.

The score remained tied until full-time and up until the end of extra-time.

England, as is our wont, then lost a penalty shoot-out to exit the tournament.

Despite the disappointment, the nation felt it had discovered a global superstar in young Michael Owen.

As for Liverpool fans, we felt like we'd just *lost* a local hero. No longer the preserve of Reds supporters, he was now the country's to love and cherish.

Did we ever forgive him?

No. I don't think we did.

CHAPTER EIGHTEEN

The Liverpool chairman and majority shareholder was David Moores, heir-apparent of the Littlewoods retail and catalogue fortune. His father had been the owner of Everton football club, and the family were steeped in both the city and the game.

David Moores took over at Anfield in 1991. He had been the one to wield the axe on Graeme Souness, at a club not known for sending their managers up the road. The last one to have been given their marching orders was Don Welsh in 1956. When I say the last, I also mean the first. Liverpool had never sacked a manager in their history up until that point. Don's 'crime' was to have seen his team relegated, the first time that Liverpool had dropped out of the top-flight for over 50 years. Even then, he was given time to turn it around.

He had two more seasons in which to try to return the club to the first division. Failing both times, he was let go. Souness was just the second manager that Liverpool had ever sacked.

Now David Moores is both a Liverpool man and a Liverpool fan. He'd once been married to a former Miss World, who also happened to be a Littlewoods' model.

He was down to earth, and was just as likely to be found on the terraces at an away game as he was in a boardroom meeting. He simply loved the team whose fortunes he had a duty to direct.

The club were still a global name, kids all over the world were still drawn to them, and many young adults had grown up supporting them because of their unparalleled success.

With the increased coverage and commercial opportunities presented by the invention of the Premier League, the team were in danger of falling behind, both on the pitch and off it.

Change was needed.

No doubt with one eye on Highbury and Arsene Wenger's influence, plus the French national team winning the World Cup on home soil in the summer of 1998, Liverpool appointed Gerard Houllier as joint first-team manager, to work alongside Roy Evans.

Ronnie Moran had retired, and you couldn't just sack a loyal servant like Evans, even if recent results were not up to hopes and expectations. Especially when we'd sacked a total of two managers in 106 years. We were not that kind of club.

Similarly, you couldn't put someone like Houllier in a subordinate position.

A compromise or – to be more precise – a cop-out, was reached.

I'll go on record right now and say that I love, absolutely love Mr Houllier. Everything you'll read in the next few chapters will have that mark of respect.

He started out as a schoolteacher, and while he was studying for that career, spent a year in Liverpool, from 1969 to 1970, teaching at Alsop school in Walton, about half a mile from Goodison, and a mile from Anfield.

Incidentally, that's my wife's alma-mater too.

He went to watch Liverpool one night, standing on the Kop, as they trounced Irish underdogs Dundalk by ten goals to nil.

Houllier was hooked.

He began his management career in France, leading minnows Nœux-les-Mines to two successive promotions before moving to Lens, where he led them into the top flight and a UEFA Cup qualifying place. He then went on to manage Paris St-Germain, where he lifted the league title in his second season in charge.

He was then chosen as Technical Director of the French Football Federation in 1988, and managed the national team for a short spell from 1992 to 1994.

Failure to qualify for the 1994 World Cup saw Houllier tender his resignation, but his talents had been well-and-truly spotted, and he was simply moved back upstairs into the Technical Director's role.

He was privy to, and indeed directly responsible for, a lot of the groundwork that led to France becoming World Champions in 1998 and European Champions two years later.

He knew all of the players – present, and up-and-coming – and was simply a mine of information of all things French, English, and European.

And he loved Liverpool.

We simply had to take him on board.

But alongside Roy?

It was never going to work.

Our playboy footballers – part-athletes, part-models – were trying to fit in all of the commercial opportunities that were coming their way.

Their agents, the more slippery ones anyway, were dangling large cheques in their faces, of which they would get their 10 or 20 percent.

'Can you skip training and come and do a photo-shoot for so-and-so. They're offering ten grand for a morning's work?'

Who is the player going to ask for permission? Roy Evans or Gerard Houllier?

I believe the lax regime went something like this.

Houllier turns up to take training.

'Where's the goalie? Where's the left-back? Where's the striker?'

'Oh, they asked me for the morning off, and I said yes.'

Daggers across the training ground. Two different philosophies at play.

In order to turn these underachievers into trophy winners, steel would need to be added, but if the players had an out (i.e., the softer of the two managers) whenever pressure was applied, what were the chances of success?

Precisely none.

By November, Roy Evans had resigned. A good man. A great Liverpool man. But two into one don't go.

And what had the new league campaign brought?

For a start, there were a few ins and outs, in terms of transfers.

In came striker Sean Dundee and midfielder Vegard Heggem. Their combined fees came to £5.3 million. The former played just three times for the club, with each appearance from the subs bench. He scored no goals, and was moved on after a year.

I once saw him in the centre of Liverpool, driving a bright yellow Porsche convertible sports car. I think it's fair to say that I saw him behind the wheel of that car more than I ever did on the pitch.

Vegard Heggem cost £3.5 million of that pre-season outlay. We were probably propping up the Gross National Product of Norway at that point. He would stay at Anfield for five seasons, yet make only 54 appearances in that time, netting three times.

He had struggled with injuries, and had arrived for a huge fee that may have raised expectations amongst the watching fans, yet he will probably be best remembered as the man who gave way on the pitch to the inaugural appearance of a young academy graduate named Steven Gerrard.

Back to the other Gerard – Monsieur Houllier – who finally had hold of the reins come November of 1998. The season was already well underway, but we'd been inconsistent for a few years by now. The few months under two different managers could hardly be anything else.

Three wins and a draw in our first four games had then turned to dross.

Three draws and two defeats in our next five games meant we could already stop dreaming of a league title. In October!

We beat Nottingham Forest by five goals to one in our next match, with Michael Owen scoring four, and then lost the next three, including consecutive home defeats to Derby County and Leeds United.

We weren't even nearly men. It's a wonder anyone even knew who we were!

We then won two, lost two, and then won three on the bounce to take us up to the end of the calendar year.

January brought more transfer activity. Houllier now had sole charge.

He brought in Jean-Michel Ferri and Rigobert Song. Together, they cost £4.3 million. Song lasted almost two years, played 34 games, and was sold to West Ham. We did, however, recoup almost of our outlay.

Ferri played just twice for Liverpool. He came on both times as a substitute, clocking up just 47 minutes in his Anfield career. He left after a year. Again, we recovered almost all of our outlay.

If Houllier was struggling to pick a winner, he was certainly adept at selling them on afterwards.

One to leave was Jason McAteer. Bought for £4 million from Bolton, he moved to Blackburn Rovers, now managed by (am I going around in circles?) Graeme Souness for £4.5 million.

The team might be stagnating, but the books were balancing all the same.

In the league, we were already also-rans. We were also out of the League Cup and the UEFA Cup. And then we were paired with Man Utd in the FA Cup at the end of January.

It was a fourth-round tie, away from home, and I watched it in a pub in Aintree, close to where my parents live.

Michael Owen scored after three minutes. For the next 85 minutes, the score remained the same.

Man Utd were miles better than us at the time. They were serial winners. We were the men in white suits. We flattered to deceive. But we were still the most bitter of rivals. When we were great, and they were shite, they'd still raised their game against us to occasionally piss on our parade. Could we do the same to them, now that they had the upper-hand?

With two minutes to go, the TV screen in the pub shut down. This was early days in the era of satellite technology. Maybe they had a dodgy box, or a dodgy subscription.

Whatever. The screen went blank. We were two minutes from knocking Man Utd out of the FA Cup.

Hearts were in mouths.

This was the age of Fergie-time, where he would always beseech a referee to play another minute or two of extra-time if the result wasn't going his way, knowing teams would always crumble in the end.

We were two minutes, plus Fergie-time, from victory.

But we had no idea what was going on.

There were no mobile phones, unless you were a yuppie or a drug dealer. The internet was in its infancy. We just needed the telly to come back on. Old-school shit like that.

It did.

The score read Man Utd 2. Liverpool 1.

In the two minutes that the television had gone out of action, United had equalised and then gone ahead. And that's how it ended.

Seriously. Maybe all of the TV sets in the land had gone blank and Ferguson had rearranged the scoreboard in our absence. I wouldn't have put it past him.

Anyway, back to the league.

We drew five, won six, and lost seven of our remaining fixtures.

Man Utd won the league. Arsenal finished second. We were seventh.

It meant no European football the following season, but that was not necessarily a bad thing.

Unless you qualified for one of the two Champions League places, the demands of the other European competitions – for which you would be eligible by finishing third, fourth, fifth, or even sixth – were quite onerous.

Who fancies an away trip to Russia or Ukraine on a Thursday night ahead of a league game on a Sunday? Answer: no-one in their right mind.

Houllier had been eased in on someone else's coat-tails. No-one would judge him on this season, as he'd shared control for a part of it, and this still was not his team.

He'd have a close season to make some changes and, in the campaign to come, he would not have the added distraction of European competition to contend with. He'd probably have been bored with it anyway. He'd practically written the rule-book on it.

Another disappointing season had come to an end. Another trophy-less, barren wilderness in the gilded history of Liverpool Football Club.

We'd made a change, and we were trying to move with the times.

We had one man at the helm – a Frenchman at that – but one with a big Scouse heart.

CHAPTER NINETEEN

Out with the old and in with the new. It was as true for the players as it was with the managers.

Since taking sole hold of the reins in November of the previous season, following the departure of Roy Evans, Gerard Houllier was now running the store.

Despite the disappointing seventh-placed finish at the end of the previous campaign, Houllier now had the opportunity to stamp his mark on proceedings.

This he certainly did. Out went the likes of David James, Paul Ince, Sean Dundee, and Oyvind Leonhardsen. In came Sander Westerveld in goal, centre-backs Stephane Henchoz and Sami Hyppia, midfielder Dietmar Hamann, and forwards Vladimir Smicer and Titi Camara.

Disappointingly, we lost Steve McManaman to Real Madrid, not even recouping a fee for a player whose contract had been allowed to run out. A shockingly bad piece of business all round for one of the most talented players of his generation. It was our loss, and The Galacticos gain.

At first, Madrid fans couldn't make out what to think of their new signing from Merseyside. They nicknamed him 'The Postman' because of his habit of delivering the ball to his team-mates 'all over the place'. He was egoless, would do the donkey-work, and simply carried the ball from A to B.

Soon, they would call him Bambi, because of his long legs and gangly, almost awkward way of running. They soon came to love him, though. He won two La Liga titles and two Champions League winners medals, with man-of-the-match performances in both finals. He made the whole Galacticos team tick. He remains one of the finest English exports ever to play on the continent.

As for The Reds, we were making wholesale changes.

Now I don't wish to be accused of hypocrisy here or of employing double-standards. I've earlier stated that I thought Graeme Souness made too many changes and all too quickly. The difference here is that Souness had inherited a title-winning side.

I don't buy the argument that the team were ageing or past their best. John Barnes, the star of the show, was in his prime at the time, at 28 years of age and would spend a further six years at the club after Souness took charge.

Houllier took over a team who hadn't won a trophy in four years, and that was the League Cup, the least significant of the three English football competitions. Change was most-definitely needed this time around.

The net spend in the summer of 1999 was close to £15 million, but the quality in the team and the squad improved immeasurably.

After a free-scoring pre-season, Liverpool bagged their first three points of the new campaign in the opening game away to Sheffield Wednesday. Fowler scored after 75 minutes with a terrific lob over Wednesday keeper Pavel Srnicek, after a great through ball from attacking midfielder Vladimir Smicer. An international compatriot of Patrick Berger, the two men were said to be great pals off the pitch.

The Kop had already coined a song for him.

'He's Czech. He's great. He's Paddy Berger's mate. Vladimir. Vladimir!'

Titi Camara then fired in a second goal with just six minutes to go. Although the Sheffield side pulled one back, close to full-time, it was too little too late, and The Reds hung on for the win.

Camara was a Guinean international, signed from Marseille for £2.6 million. Though many outside of Anfield failed to recognise his talents, he was adored by the Liverpool-faithful, becoming a cult-hero and providing many highlights for the fans in his all-too-short stay at the club.

He was raw and original, and the crowd saw something in him that they truly tuned into. An enthusiastic refrain of 'Tee, Tee, Tee, Tee-Tee. Tee, Tee, Tee, Tee-Tee. Tee, Tee, Tee, Tee-Tee. Tee, Tee, Tee Camara' would ring out, and he would be off. He would try literally anything.

On the half-way line facing his own goal, he'd just whack the ball over his head and go and chase it, turning the entire opposition team around and causing the whole ground to get to their feet as they cheered him on in amazement and with unbridled joy. He was just electric. Unorthodox. Probably crazy. But crazy-good. And we loved him.

My young niece has one of those baby books. 'My first word was' etc.

Her first song was the Titi Camara one. He should have stayed and become a club legend. Instead, he just got himself off to a fine start.

There was certainly an air of expectancy and excitement in the stands. In the years since stability deserted us, back in 1991, we had been a little punch-drunk on the ropes.

Now we had our own Gallic general at the helm. His credentials, both at league level and internationally were quite impeccable. Technical

Football Director for the team that has just won the World Cup! It doesn't get much better than that.

Our average attendances at Anfield appeared to go up as a result of the increased expectation. We hadn't averaged more than 40,000 spectators at our homes games since 1980. This was partially a result of changes from standing to seating in various parts of the ground. In more recent seasons, we had failed to reach full capacity as a result of our quality and efforts on the pitch.

In Houllier's first full season in sole charge of the club, we would surpass 43,000 as our average home-crowd.

Could the team deliver what the crowds wanted: a competitive, combative squad of talented footballers capable of bringing the silverware the fans so craved?

Houllier had signed a five-year contract when he had first joined The Reds. His first year was spent in partnership with Roy Evans before seeing out the rest of the season alone.

He now had four years left to make the manager's position his own and to restore the Anfield club to its former glory.

The clock was ticking. The fans were watching. The season was already underway.

One of Houllier's first acts upon taking over was to ask the club to find him a new assistant. With a certain 'laissez-faire' attitude, his only stipulation was that they should find him somebody with a Liverpool heart.

A call was put out to Phil Thompson, a footballing man who fit the bill to perfection. In a distinguished playing career with the club that he had watched from the Kop as a boy, Thompson collected 16 major trophies in 13 years, including seven league titles and three European Cups. If you were to make an England all-star XI based on silverware alone, Thompson is probably in there.

He'd previously come on board as a coach at Liverpool under Kenny Dalglish in 1986, and remained with the club when Souness took over, eventually leaving in 1993 under something of a cloud. Apparently, Souness heard whispers that Thompson was moaning about the atmosphere and the regression at Anfield under the new regime.

Thompson, as I guess is only right, was forced to resign, but not before his good work in the role had been noted by the directors and the higher-ups at the club.

After a 5-a-side workout, alongside some old team-mates (not your average game of 5-a-side I'm sure, in terms of quality!), Phil realised he'd had a missed-call from LFC.

He knew they wouldn't be calling just to catch up on old times.

When he returned the phone call, he was told that Gerard Houllier was looking for an assistant manager. They'd thought of him. Would he be interested? (I'm thinking bear, excrement, and lots of trees at this point).

So Thompson came on board the Gerard Houllier Express. And the result – for a while at least – was something approaching magical.

CHAPTER TWENTY

Paul Ince was gone, sold to Middlesbrough for a million quid. Houllier claimed to be an admirer of his ability, but felt he was a little too overbearing in his presence. The younger lads in the dressing room were too attendant on his opinions, and too eager to accept his social invitations.

What Houllier needed was a squad focussed solely on him and his staff and his planned-direction for the club, which involved a steep and completely-upwardly mobile trajectory. He wanted the players' full attention in order to be able to drive the team forward.

Jamie Redknapp was appointed the club's new captain. Robbie Fowler was made vice-captain.

We had a new goalie, a new centre-back pairing, and – in Didi Hamann – a world-class defensive midfielder protecting the back four.

We might not win the league this season, but we'd be nobody's fool either.

First game, first win. We were up and running.

After Sheffield Wednesday came newly-promoted Watford, the club who had previously given us our left-wing wizard John Barnes.

No longer in the giving-mood, The Hornets beat us 1-0 at Anfield to puncture our early-season optimism.

This was followed by another defeat, away to Middlesbrough, and again by a score-line of one goal to nil. I failed to make the trip this time, my fleeting personal relationship – of the season before – having gone by the way-side. Such is life.

We then won our next two matches, the first away to Leeds, with Camara again on the scoresheet, and then at home to Arsenal with goals from Fowler and Berger.

At the end of the opening month of the season, after five Premier League matches, we were in a nothing-to-write-home-about eighth place. Not great, but possibly lying in wait.

Next up was a home game against Man Utd. We lost 3-2 in a game in which Carragher found the back of the net twice. The back of his *own* net twice. I bet Gary Neville slept well that night, even if Jamie didn't.

The next four matches for Liverpool must go down as some sort of record, for they contained between them no fewer than seven red cards!

First came an away draw at Leicester City, in which Owen bagged a brace. Frank Sinclair saw red for Leicester in that game after a foul on Titi Camara that saw our Guinean forward leave the field injured as a result.

Next up was a memorable Merseyside derby. Memorable for all the wrong reasons. For one, we lost by one goal to nil. A Kevin Campbell goal with just four minutes on the clock, and 86 minutes of normal time still to play.

Chasing the game, Houllier had made all of his available three substitutions by the 70th minute.

One thing I loved about Houllier was his decisiveness. If we were drawing a game after 60 minutes, he'd make a switch and on would go a substitute. Often, we'd be ahead within a few minutes of that forward-thinking move.

Here, it back-fired.

In the 75th minute, Franny Jeffers of Everton and Liverpool keeper Westerveld got involved in a brawl that saw both players sent to the stands. With no more cards left to play, The Reds spent the last 15 minutes reduced to ten men and with full-back Steve Staunton doing his best between the sticks to keep The Toffees at bay.

Then Steven Gerrard got in on the act and was sent for an early bath after a waist-high challenge on the Blues' goal-scorer, Campbell.

Despite six minutes of injury-time to be played, accumulated for all of the game's incidents, the nine men of Liverpool couldn't equalise against the ten men of Everton.

Then came a 0-0 draw away at Aston Villa. Steve Staunton, our surrogate-goalie from the derby match saw red in this one. I remember it well.

One time, just a couple of years earlier, I'd been having a tough time at work.

I could do nothing right in my boss's eyes. Other colleagues would be doing exactly the same things as me, and nothing would be said. I, though, seemed to have a target on my back.

I mentioned my frustration to my sister. She's a schoolteacher. She explained things like this.

'Sometimes, people wind you up. The red mist comes over you. The kid right next to that one might be doing exactly the same thing, but you can't see it. Your focus and your animosity has a single trajectory.'

Just as my boss had it in for me, Steve Staunton had the same thing going on in this game against Villa. The referee could see no-one and nothing but him. In the referee's eyes, Staunton appeared to be up to no good, and not playing fair.

But he had done nothing wrong. Nothing whatsoever.

In return, the referee's unwarranted focus was winding Staunton up. Why me? He seemed to be saying.

Then the ref gave a free-kick against Staunton.

The Liverpool wall had to retreat ten yards.

The Villa player taking the kick then knocked the ball about six inches to one side to a team-mate who was standing beside him.

They were trying to take a quick one. Trying to be a bit clever.

Staunton was on his game. He was fired up. He was the only one in our defensive wall to spot that quick sleight-of-hand nudge of the ball.

He came sprinting forward to block whatever action was about to take place, because the ball was now in play.

The referee wasn't watching the play. He could only see Staunton. He had that 'teacher-versus-naughty-school-kid' focus. He genuinely thought that Staunton had lost the plot. Gone feral. He didn't want him on his football pitch a minute longer. Already shown a yellow card for the initial foul, he now showed Stevie a red.

Only when he watched the replay later that night or the next day did the referee realise his mistake and rescind the red card. By then, it was too late.

In a match that we looked like we might go on to win, when we went down – unfairly– to ten men, we could merely hold on for the draw.

Thanks for the belated apology, ref, but we'd have rather have had the points.

In our next game, we faced Chelsea, who had beaten the mighty Man Utd by five goals to nil in their previous fixture.

It was to be another action-packed match, in which The Reds emerged one-nil victors courtesy of a goal from David Thompson, while Michael Owen also missed a penalty that would have given us a more convincing score-line. Marcel Desailly and serial-offender and wind-up merchant Dennis Wise were sent off in the fixture for the Londoners.

By mid-October, Liverpool were ninth in the league, eight points behind the early-season front-runners Leeds United.

Injuries to Fowler and Owen then left The Reds looking lightweight up the pitch for the next run of matches.

The burden of leading the forward-line would rest on Camara's shoulders, while he had major problems of his own, of a personal kind.

More than 3,000 miles away, back in his birthplace of Conakry in Guinea, Titi's father had fallen seriously ill. Any normal son, any normal person, would have left their place of work to be by the old man's bedside in case things were to turn out for the worse.

But, putting the needs of the team and the club before his own, and with amazing fortitude, Titi toughed it out.

At a midweek game against Southampton at the Dell, with The Reds trailing to a first-half Saints goal, Camara popped up with a late equaliser to earn us a point.

Then, in a home match against West Ham four days later, Camara scored the only goal of the game to give Liverpool the victory.

Titi's father had passed away the day before. Everyone in the stadium had heard the news. Camara hadn't gone back to say his last goodbyes, and he wouldn't even make the funeral. Instead, he had chosen to stay behind and play for us.

When he scored that winning goal against The Hammers, he immediately dropped to his knees in front of the Kop, held his head in his hands, and cried.

I hope he felt our love that day, coming from every spectator in the ground. He certainly deserved it.

Though his time at the club would ultimately be all-too-brief, he had made a huge impression.

Former Reds hero David Fairclough described him as 'swashbuckling'. Jamie Carragher, in the same Anfield podcast ('100 players who shook the Kop'), said that for the first three or four months of Camara's Liverpool career, he thought that we had signed Pele! He was unstoppable, unplayable, and unbelievable.

Camara then scored again in his next outing, as Liverpool beat Bradford to move up to sixth in the table.

Since losing to Everton in that ill-tempered derby, The Reds had gone five games unbeaten. Manager Gerard Houllier told the BBC after this latest win that he now wanted five more. He added, 'We were not good at the beginning (of the match). I want my team to take the game by the scruff of the neck, but we were too soft, too gentle, too nice, and you have to be more aggressive at this level.'

It seemed that Liverpool were going to be pushovers no longer. The team were improving – slowly but surely – and it seemed as if the man at the helm was providing the clear direction that our underachieving team so desperately needed.

Not only was he not content with recent results, as fine as they were, he was demanding more of the same. And then some.

In the next spell of games, the team almost delivered what Houllier had asked for, winning four of their next five matches. The run of victories also provided a debut goal for Steven Gerrard in a 4-1 win over Sheffield Wednesday.

Along with Steven Gerrard, David Thompson and Danny Murphy also scored in that match. The trio were all born within a 30-mile radius of Anfield, and the BBC reported that 'Liverpool's home-grown youngsters came of age with an impressive display.'

They went on to say that it was 'a classy victory that in large parts displayed the best of Houllier's Anfield revolution.' As if that wasn't enough, they also added that 'the foreign imports combined sweetly with the hungry youngsters in a blend of style and passion that Liverpool supporters have been craving for some time.'

The result took the team up to fifth in the Premiership.

People were starting to take notice of our forward momentum.

A Michael Owen brace in an away draw at Newcastle, was then followed by a 3-1 home win against Wimbledon.

And that brought the calendar year 1999 to a close.

There were signs for optimism that the ten-year drought that we had endured might soon be over. The nineties had largely been a write-off in a footballing sense, but we looked well-placed as we entered the new millennium with our new manager, Gerard Houllier.

We had a new and improved team, and it appeared that we also had a winning mentality to go with it.

CHAPTER TWENTY-ONE

Three wins, a draw, and one defeat in the league saw Liverpool move up to third place by mid-February in the 1999/2000 season. Slowly, incrementally, we were closing in on the leading pack.

In March, Houllier splashed out £11 million on Emile Ivanhoe Heskey from Leicester City. We had Owen, Fowler, and Camara doing the business up front, the latter showing his character by scoring the only goal in an away victory at Highbury. Others, however, such as Erik Meijer, had failed to hold down a place up front.

Man Utd had four decent centre-forwards in Sheringham, Solskjaer, Cole and Yorke. Gerard Houllier obviously felt that we should have the same, especially after Fowler and Owen had been absent through injury for large parts of the season.

Plus, and this became apparent as the seasons went on, Michael Owen – as great and prolific as he was – could benefit from someone big and powerful alongside him.

Defenders, especially bruising central defenders, marked Owen out for special treatment. They weren't about to let him have things all his own way. They would get stuck into him to try to put him off his game.

Heskey would give them it back. Sometimes he'd give it to them before they even got theirs in. He was that type of player. I'll eulogise about him in due course. Suffice it to say (for now) that he was the bodyguard that the young and slightly-built Owen needed, as well as a decent player in his own right.

After scoring a brace in an away win at Wimbledon, Houllier had this to say about his new centre-forward Heskey, no doubt with one eye on those sniping at either the size of the fee or the quality of the player himself. 'There are a lot of sceptical attitudes, but we know what he contributes and what he brings to us. There is no pressure for Emile to score. The most important thing is that the team wins.'

And win we did. As March became April, Liverpool were second in the league, though still a long way behind the leaders Man Utd.

There were three Champions League places up for grabs that year. The Reds looked certain to take one of them. Not the one we wanted, the prize for finishing first, but it would be a further statement of intent if we were going to be mixing it with the best of Europe the following season.

There were five games of the league campaign still to go, and five teams competing for the two remaining spots in Europe's top footballing competition: Leeds, Chelsea, Arsenal, Aston Villa, and ourselves.

Then, as April turned to May, Liverpool went to pieces, losing three and drawing two of our remaining fixtures.

Man Utd were title-winners. Arsenal were second. Leeds United were third.

Liverpool trailed home in fourth position. No Champions League place for us. We would have to be content with a UEFA Cup place instead.

Yet, as things transpired, this was not as disappointing as it sounds.

We had fared badly in the domestic competitions this season, with a third-round exit in the League Cup and a fourth-round exit in the FA Cup.

But, under the surface, things were bubbling away.

Houllier had bought well the previous close-season, and had then added to the team with the arrival of Heskey when the last campaign was well underway.

What did the manager have up his sleeve for this summer's transfer activity? Could he repeat or even improve on his earlier success in the marketplace?

We were about to find out, and it would not be long before the word 'winners' began to crop up after the name Liverpool. The good times were about to roll.

Houllier again bought wisely, adding experience to the squad to complement the talents of his burgeoning young stars.

He'd put Heskey in alongside Owen towards the back-end of the previous season, and that partnership had produced instant dividends.

So much so, in fact, that Titi Camara saw the writing on the wall. He'd been our third-choice striker, but he had done well enough to inch his way up the pecking order and possibly command a starting place, even ahead of Fowler and Owen, or so he believed.

Then Heskey had joined the club and Camara was back at square one.

To be honest, his performances had been so electric that you can't blame the lad for wanting to be out there every week, hearing the 'Tee-Tee, Tee-Tee-Tee' song belting out. Who wouldn't love a bit of that?

He could have kept his head down and waited for opportunities to play. After all, there'd been plenty of those the season before when injuries had started to bite.

He'd have been under no pressure from the fans, and he could have enjoyed all of the adoration that the supporters sincerely felt for him.

Possibly believing the hype that our adulation inspired in him, he suddenly decided to continue his career elsewhere.

Sometimes, a player is just right for a club, for a team, for a fan-base, and everything gels. There's no guarantee that the same things will all fall into place somewhere else.

Camara moved to West Ham. We recouped our full transfer fee for him, but sadly things didn't work out well for him at The Hammers. He would make only 14 appearances in a little over two years with the London club. They never understood what we ever saw in him. If he had just bitten his tongue and stayed with us, I'm sure the whole world would have got to know his name. But it wasn't to be.

Also to leave Liverpool that summer was goalkeeper Brad Friedel, who moved to Blackburn on a free transfer. Unlucky not to have been given a proper run in the team at Anfield, he was then held up as a scapegoat – when it really wasn't his fault – for a defeat at Man Utd where the referee awarded the softest of penalties in a 1-0 defeat.

A speculative shot from Solskjaer from 25 yards had bobbled awkwardly and squirmed under Brad Friedel's body, going out for a corner.

Beckham sent in the corner, and Brad punched the ball up in the air, not quite convincingly, it has to be said.

There was lots of pushing and shoving in the box. As the ball came down, it hit Jason McAteer on the arm as he was being pulled and harried by Paul Scholes.

McAteer was just trying to hold him at bay. It was definitely not a handball. But, at Old Trafford, what United wanted, they always seemed to get.

And you can't expect the keeper to save a pen but, from that day on, Friedel seemed to have a question mark over him that he could never quite shake, and his Anfield days were numbered. He never got the chance to prove the doubters wrong.

I remember my dad saying, when we bought him, that you couldn't really go wrong with an American keeper. Although the country wasn't known as a haven of 'soccer', all of the games that they play involve the hands. Baseball, Basketball, American Football. So, from an early age, a kid is used to using his hands in sport. I guess that makes sense.

I was pleased that Friedel was finally able to show English football supporters what a class act he truly was. He's another one that we should have kept, and he could have been – as he was for Blackburn – our first-choice keeper for the next ten years.

We moved a few others on too. Phil Babb and Steve Staunton from our defensive line-up, and David Thomson from midfield. The latter had apparently fallen out with the assistant manager, Phil Thompson. While the player's talent was never in question, his attitude was, and he moved to Coventry City for a fee of almost £3 million. He later scored for the Sky Blues against Man Utd, so there'll always be a place for him in our hearts.

Ultimately, ten members of the squad were to go that summer, with the same number coming in. One was Nick Barmby, who joined from Everton for £6 million. Walter Smith, the Blue's manager at the time said that Barmby had uttered the words that no Evertonian ever wanted to hear, which were 'I want to play for Liverpool!'

Joining Barmby were German international full-backs Christian Ziege and Markus Babbel. That was the defence sorted.

Igor Biscan, a six-foot three central-midfielder joined from Dinamo Zagreb, having been courted by Barcelona, Juventus, Ajax, and AC Milan. Having lost one cult-favourite in Camara, Biscan would go on to be another over the course of five full seasons with The Reds.

Up front, we brought in Jari Litmanen. Voted the greatest Finnish footballer of all-time, he had won the Champions League with Ajax in 1995, where he was also the competition's top-scorer that season, before later moving to Barcelona.

His nickname at Ajax was 'The Professor' for his in-depth knowledge of the game. For the fans, he was 'Merlin' for his wizardry on the pitch. He was also an ice-cold master from the 12-yard spot, converting 28 of the 29 penalties that he took throughout his career.

After signing the exalted Finn, Houllier said, "He is a world-class player. He comes with a massive reputation and I believe he's one of the most exciting signings we have made."

Litmanen was also a lifelong Reds fan. His favourite player was Kenny Dalglish.

Not shy, and not fazed by the weight of expectation that it might bring, he asked to be given the number seven shirt, as worn by The King. Unfortunately, that had already been taken by Vladimir Smicer. Numbers 17 and 27 were also in use, so Jari chose number 37. As long as it had that number seven in there somewhere, he was happy.

Another major arrival that summer was 35-year-old Gary McAllister, who joined the club on a free transfer from Coventry.

A Premier League winner with Leeds United, McAllister was a player's player. He was a midfield-maestro, and simply one of the finest footballers of the modern era.

He'd formed a close bond with fellow Scot Gordon Strachan, the pair moving from Leeds to Coventry together and continuing to defy the years with their guile and talent and their will-to-win.

A severe injury robbed McAllister of almost a year of football at the age of 32. It might have seemed like a disappointing end to his career. Instead, it actually prolonged it.

Following that long lay-off and rest, Gary returned to form and fitness and was ever-present in his last league campaign with the Sky Blues before Liverpool came calling.

Already boasting the likes of Didi Hamann in midfield, along with Jamie Redknapp, Danny Murphy, and Steven Gerrard, not to mention our attacking midfielders from the Czech Republic Patrick Berger and Vladimir Smicer, and newcomers Barmby and Biscan, any seasoned informer might reasonably have asked why we needed the veteran McAllister. Where would we play him? Would he even get a game?

It just goes to show that you can never have too much of a good thing, because use him we did, and need him we did. Time and time again.

Things were about to get heady. Things were about to get (to use a phrase used in the aftermath) unprecedented.

To negotiate these uncharted waters, in recent times at least, we would need a voice of experience, a real leader, and a real talent at that. McAllister was it.

The squad had been improved immeasurably the season before. The latest additions simply built on those foundations, and we now had strength in depth.

But so far under Houllier we'd won nothing, and in taking on the might of Arsenal and Man Utd, it appeared that we still had a mountain to climb.

And yet, though no-one dared predict it, or even to dream it, Liverpool Football Club were about to enjoy their most successful season in years.

For the expectant fans, the loyal Anfield-faithful, it couldn't come a day too soon.

CHAPTER TWENTY-TWO

Our 2000/2001 league season started with a home win over Bradford, courtesy of a lone strike from Ivanhoe Heskey.

We were then brought back down to earth when we lost 2-0 away at Arsenal.

Our form for the rest of August and right through September can best be described as inconsistent, with three draws and two wins before a 3-0 capitulation at Chelsea on the 1st of October.

A victory in that last game would have sent us up to second place in the table. Instead, the result lifted Chelsea out of the relegation zone and served as a reality check for The Reds.

The remainder of the month showed a marked improvement as we hit back with three wins on the bounce. Heskey bagged a hat-trick in the first of those matches, before he got the winner against his old club Leicester, and then opened the scoring in the Merseyside derby. He was in a rich vein of form.

November was disappointing, with only one win in three. We did, however, manage goals in each of those games, and Heskey had got his name on the score-sheet a further three times.

December produced another mixed-bag: a trio of victories and a brace of defeats. Danny Murphy had bagged the winner away at Old Trafford to begin what was a remarkable set of results against the old enemy – United – under Gerard Houllier.

This was Man Utd's first league reversal at home in two years. The victory was made all the sweeter for Liverpool fans as it came from a free-kick awarded against Gary Neville, the serial Scouse-baiter.

A long ball up-field should have been easy for Neville to control. He had all the time in the world to chest the ball down, even if it did bounce up in front of him a little awkwardly.

He was in yards of space, and under no pressure whatsoever, but rather than coping with the awkward ball, he took the weight off it using both of his forearms, and then had the temerity to look astounded when the ref blew up for handball.

His misery was compounded when Murphy curled the resulting free-kick into the top corner.

We had won a game at the home of our deadly foe, but there was little chance of us winning the league that year. United were already well clear at the top. At the end of the 2000, Liverpool were a modestly-placed sixth.

January and February brought three wins and three draws and saw us move up the table, but Man Utd were miles out in front, of us and everyone else.

Earlier in the campaign, back in September, I had been full of optimism about our progress under Houllier and the improvements that he'd made to the team.

My dad's birthday was coming up. He always liked a bet, and I thought I'd go and stick a tenner on for him.

I think we were about 8/1 to win the league at the time. There was also another bet being advertised in the bookies when I popped in. Liverpool to win all three cup competitions for which they were entered: the League Cup, the FA Cup, and the UEFA Cup. The odds were 50 to 1.

Don't be daft, I told myself. It's never been done before. No-one wins three cups in one season.

I gave my dad his birthday card with a £10 betting slip inside with Liverpool to win the league.

As we neared the end of February, the dream of winning the league was already over, forgotten for another season.

The cup dream, however, was still in play. There would be challenges ahead, right up to the last minute of the last game in those competitions, but we had our first final on the horizon.

With Wembley undergoing reconstruction, the Millennium Stadium in Cardiff was the setting. The League Cup was the prize on offer. Birmingham City were the opposition.

It was our first appearance in a cup final for five years. Reds fans clamoured to be there. I was one of them.

A gang of us left Liverpool in a mini-bus for the long drive to South Wales. We spent the night before the game in a guesthouse, then made our way to the arena the following day.

Birmingham played their football in the division below us. Many observers thought the cup was ours for the taking.

The underdogs, however, had other ideas.

For the opening 30 minutes, the teams were evenly-matched before a piece of Fowler magic put Liverpool ahead.

A long ball up-field from Stephane Henchoz was then flicked on by the head of Heskey.

The ball bounced up nicely and, spotting the Birmingham keeper off his line, Fowler put his boot through it, sending the ball in a trajectory that resembled the new Wembley arch!

It went up in the air, sailed over the keeper, and flew into the back of the net from 30 yards out – a magnificent goal, worthy of winning any cup final.

Except, deep into injury-time in the match, Birmingham won a penalty which they converted to take the game into extra-time.

Thirty minutes later, with both sides having had chances to score but failing to break the deadlock, the final was set to be decided on a penalty shoot-out.

McAllister scored first for Liverpool. Birmingham then missed their opening pen to hand the advantage to The Reds.

Barmby and Ziege scored theirs to keep Liverpool's noses out in front, while Birmingham netted their next two to put the pressure back on us.

Hamann missed his, and they scored theirs, which meant we were now all-tied once more.

Both teams successfully converted the last of the five pens, meaning we were about to enter the sudden-death phase.

Up stepped Jamie Carragher.

I was right behind the goal.

'What's he doing taking it?' I thought. 'He's a defender. *Anyone* but him.'

He scored. An assured and confident strike.

Sander Westerveld then saved from future-Evertonian Andy Johnson to send Liverpool into raptures.

We had won. It was only the League Cup, *but it was a trophy*! And we still had two others to play for.

The nay-sayers said 'It was only Birmingham. League One opposition. You were expected to win.'

And they may have had a point, except no-one just picks you up and plonks you in the final. You have to get there.

Our journey had been memorable and remarkable in so many ways.

We began back in early November, with a midweek game against Chelsea. We had scored through Danny Murphy before the Londoners equalised through Zola.

It was an ill-tempered match, and Houllier replaced the much-slighter figure of Smicer with Emile Heskey with 18 minutes of normal time to go and the match still evenly-tied.

For as long as I live, I will never forget Heskey's performance that night. Though only a cameo, he earned my everlasting appreciation.

Although a big, powerful man, Emile is softly-spoken and comes across as quite the gentleman. He was certainly no bully on the pitch.

Whatever it was that Houllier had said to him as he prepared to join the fray, it certainly did the trick. Heskey got stuck into everyone. He played like a man possessed; as if his very life depended on it. He was so fired-up, it was unbelievable.

For want of a better description, I can only say that he knocked the f*ck out of the three big Chelsea central defenders. He had Marcel Desailly, Winston Bogarde, and Mario Melchiot all pulling their hair out. They were looking at each other, thinking 'How do we handle this wrecking ball, and what have we done to upset him?!'

Heskey was booked for a waist-high challenge on Melchiot. He then helped set up the winner for Robbie Fowler, before he finally saw red and got sent-off after clashing with Bogarde in the Chelsea penalty area.

It was a late appearance and an early bath for Ivanhoe, but a performance that will live long in the memory. It was simply outstanding. The stuff of legend. Thank you Emile.

In the next round, we beat Stoke City by eight goals to nil, with six different Liverpool players getting on the score-sheet and Robbie Fowler scoring a hat-trick.

We then faced Fulham on home soil in a game which was still scoreless after 90 minutes. It took three goals in extra-time to book The Reds' place in the semi-finals.

In the first match of a two-legged tie against Crystal Palace, we lost 2-1 at Selhurst Park to set up a nervy second leg at Anfield. With the prize of a cup-final place on offer, Liverpool turned the tie around with a comfortable 5-0 win.

No-one just puts you in a final. You have to earn the right to be there. We'd certainly done that and, at the Millennium Stadium, we got our just rewards for all of our efforts.

One cup down and two still to go.

We couldn't, could we?

We most certainly could!

CHAPTER TWENTY-THREE

Our FA Cup campaign began in January with a home-tie against Rotherham. We won 3-0 with a brace from Heskey and another from Didi Hamann.

The next round saw us drawn away to Leeds United. Heskey scored again, as did Barmby, and we won by two goals to nil.

Manchester City were then the visitors to Anfield. It was testament to Liverpool's strength-in-depth that Owen and Fowler were both left out of the starting XI, with Heskey and Litmanen paired up front. After just 13 minutes play, The Reds were 2-0 up in a match that we would go on to win 4-2.

In the cup quarter-final, we were drawn against our near-neighbours Tranmere Rovers from just across the water – as we Scousers like to call it – their home ground being on the opposite bank of the River Mersey.

We knew that it would not be an easy match. Tranmere had already taken the scalps of two Premier League sides in Southampton and Everton in the previous rounds. They were the underdogs, they were confident, and it was both a cup-tie and a local derby; so anything could happen.

Houllier was asked beforehand if he knew what to expect, and how he planned to counter Tranmere's giant-killing act.

Gerard's response was a classic.

He said, 'If we had a team of Jamie Carraghers, we would win.'

He knew exactly what was needed. A bit of grit and some of that 'roll-your-sleeves-up' mentality.

We didn't have a team of Carraghers. We only had one, plus a talented squad of other individuals. Still, it was a fabulous quote, and an Anfield chant was born out of it to the tune of The Beatles' *Yellow Submarine*.

It went something like this.

Number one, is Carragher.

Number two (oo-ooh), is Carragher.

Number three, is Carragher.

And number four (or oor), is Carragher.

Carragher!

We all dream of a team of Carraghers.

A team of Carraghers. A team of Carraghers.

We all dream of a team of Carraghers.

A team of Carraghers. A team of Carraghers.

And number five…..etc etc.

You've got to love a man whose quotes become songs on The Kop.

And thus inspired, and knowing what to do, we duly dispensed with Tranmere in the tie by four goals to two.

We were now into the semi-finals and up against lower-league opposition once more, this time in the form of Wycombe Wanderers from the second division.

They had also claimed a Premiership scalp as they progressed through the competition, beating Leicester City away from home to earn the right to fight for a place in the FA Cup final.

The match was a single-tie and would be played at a neutral ground. The game still remained scoreless with almost 80 minutes gone. Then Heskey and Fowler both found the opposition net in quick succession, and the result looked to be in the bag before a late consolation goal from Wycombe sent Red hearts racing.

Thankfully, it was a case of 'too-little-too-late' for Wycombe, and Liverpool had booked their place in the FA Cup final, where we would face Arsenal; no easy task.

The date was set for Saturday the 12th of May. The setting again would be Cardiff. It would go down in history as the Michael Owen cup final, and he was about to live every young boy's dream.

It was the 119th time that the competition had been staged. It was the world's oldest knockout football tournament. It was the first time that the final had ever been held outside of England, (as we awaited new Wembley to be built) and also the first time that neither manager had come from these shores, as both Houllier and Wenger were French.

Arsenal were the 'better side' at the time. Those were Gerard Houllier's words, not mine, as told to the *Daily Telegraph*. He believed that they were more mature, more experienced, and also had more ability in certain areas.

In his pre-match team-talk, he told the players that it would be how each side responded to setbacks during the game that would decide the result.

His words worked, and The Reds went onto the pitch with the spirit that they might have to, and would be able to, overcome adversity in order to achieve victory.

Arsenal were the better side, and Liverpool were fortunate not to concede a penalty when Stephane Henchoz threw himself in the way of a goal-bound shot from Thierry Henry, with the ball bobbling up and striking the defender's arm before bouncing out for a corner.

And I'm being kind to Henchoz there. Nowadays, it's a definite pen.

We rode our luck. We stayed in the game. We had chances, but The Gunners had even more.

In the 72nd minute, Arsenal made one of them count when Freddie Ljungberg put Arsenal ahead.

Then, in the 83rd minute, McAllister swung a free-kick into the 18-yard box. An Arsenal defender attempted to clear it but merely nodded it skywards. Markus Babbel fought bravely for the ball and got his head on it, flicking it back into the danger area.

It landed at the feet of Michael Owen, who instantly spun and smacked it right-footed on the half-volley into the Arsenal net.

Game on.

With time running out, Arsenal then won a free-kick of their own in the Liverpool half of the pitch.

The ball was lofted in to the edge of the box. Most of our team were back defending the set-piece. Heskey came out of the scrum with the ball and played it to Patrick Berger, who hit a first-time 40-yard pass for Michael Owen to chase.

There are two England international defenders as well as the England goalkeeper still to beat. It's the FA Cup final. There are only two minutes to go.

Easy, yes?

Lee Dixon looked favourite to win the race, but Michael Owen wanted it more, and he got there first.

Tony Adams, the Arsenal captain, was sweeping in, coming across to intercept and halt Owen's progress. A little nudge of the ball to the left gave Michael another yard or two of space. The ball was still in his possession.

In order to move the ball out of the range of Tony Adams, Owen appeared to have dragged the ball too far out wide, creating an impossible angle.

But this was the kid whose reverse-shot across the Argentine goalie in the world Cup of '98 had been goal of the tournament. Owen hit this one left-footed, on his so-called weaker foot, right across the body of David Seaman and into the bottom right-hand corner of the goal.

Owen did a somersault in celebration. He also happened to be at the Liverpool end of the ground where our fans were going wild.

We'd turned it around. *He'd* turned it around. Snatched victory from the jaws of defeat. No extra-time was needed. We just had to hold out for two more minutes, which we did, and our second trophy of the season was in the bag.

Michael Owen later said that the game against Arsenal was the best day of his career. He went on to say that it was the game that he looked back on – more than any other – as the most exhilarating experience of his footballing career.

And, to think, just four days later, we still had another huge match to play.

This time it would be in Dortmund, Germany, where we were going to face Alaves in the UEFA Cup final.

Johan Cruyff, in the build-up to the game, said he thought it would be a dull 0-0 affair. It just goes to show what even one of the game's finest ever practitioners knows about football.

CHAPTER TWENTY-FOUR

The doubters said 'Who the effing-hell are Alaves?' Again, I answer, no-one just plonks you in a final.

The Spanish side had conquered Inter Milan en route, as well as beating Rosenberg of Norway and Rayo Vallecano of Spain. They then put nine goals past Kaiserslautern of Germany in their two-legged semi-final.

The fact that they were something of an unknown quantity did not make things any easier for us.

Our own path to the final was littered with the names of the great and the good of European football and, unlike in the Champions League, where teams could lose two or three times in the group stage and still progress, the UEFA Cup was a proper knockout competition.

You'd draw someone out of the hat and play them home and away, and the winner over the two legs would then go into the next round. Just like in the good old days.

We'd beaten Rapid Bucharest, and the Czech champions Slovan Liberec, before taking on Olympiacos of Greece. After safely negotiating those hurdles, we then faced a tough tie against Roma.

A Michael Owen double away from home set us up nicely for the second leg at Anfield where, despite losing the game by a goal to nil, Liverpool progressed to the quarter-finals, where we would face Porto, managed by the self-styled Special One, Jose Mourinho.

Three years later, Porto would go on to win the Champions League. They wouldn't be pushovers here either.

A 0-0 draw in Portugal left the tie delicately-poised. In the return leg at Anfield, despite the Portuguese team employing every continental trick in the book, goals from Danny Murphy and Michael Owen ensured that their theatrics were ultimately for nought, and it was our name that would go into the semi-finals.

Our opponents would be the mighty Barcelona.

And games didn't get much bigger than that.

The first leg was played at the Nou Camp. A star-studded Barca side, that included a young Pep Guardiola in the team, failed to penetrate a backs-to-the-wall defensive display from The Reds.

For the return fixture, Liverpool would need to do more of the same, with a solid back-line, while also ensuring that we offered a little more in attack.

Houllier selected Heskey and Owen up front. It seemed that these two were now his first-choice pairing. Even a goalscorer of Robbie Fowler's calibre could not prise his way in-between the effective Owen-Heskey double-act.

At a special European night at Anfield, a tense tie was edging its way towards half-time at 0-0 when Patrick Kluivert, the Barca striker, inexplicably handled the ball in his own box following a Liverpool corner.

The referee had no hesitation in pointing to the spot, and Gary McAllister stepped up to take the penalty.

He kept his nerve and sent the keeper the wrong way, with the ball nestling in the bottom right-hand corner of the net.

Cue delirium.

We just needed to hold on for a further 45 minutes to reach our first European final in 16 years.

And hold on we did, and how the Anfield crowd celebrated that night.

Four days after winning the FA Cup, it was over to Germany to face unheralded Alaves.

In a press conference before the match, one of the reporters posed a cheeky yet curious question to Houllier.

'Liverpool,' he said, 'are a counter-attacking team. Alaves,' he continued, 'are also a counter-attacking team. Does that mean that both teams are just going to sit in their own halves?'

Gerard Houllier simply smiled at the questioner. He had been around the game long enough to know a thing or two, and he understood what the reporter was so impishly implying.

'Yes,' said the Liverpool manager, 'maybe it will be the most boring game ever.'

Except it wasn't. The result was something quite extraordinary.

Goals from Markus Babbel and Steven Gerrard gave The Reds an early lead.

Alaves then pulled one back before a McAllister penalty leading up to the interval left Liverpool sitting pretty with a 3-1 cushion.

Within six minutes of the restart, the Spanish side were level.

Robbie Fowler was then introduced from the bench and, in the 71st minute, he put Liverpool back in front with a peach of a goal.

He ran along the edge of the 18-yard box with a wall of defenders in front of him.

He shaped to shoot, and the crowd willed him on.

'Hit it now!'

He didn't.

He moved to the right, still running with the ball, and shaped to shoot.

'Now!' came the shouts.

He didn't.

With one more touch to the right, he then let-loose, firing a right-foot shot past the keeper's outstretched arm and into the bottom corner of the net.

Fowler was mobbed, and Alaves looked defeated, but there was still plenty of drama to come.

Jordi Cruyff, once of Man Utd, equalised in the 89th minute to send the match into extra-time. Hearts back in Manchester were lifted. Johan, Jordi's dad, was left wondering what had happened to his 0-0 prediction.

Then, with just three minutes left to play before the penalty shoot-out, Alaves full-back Delfi Geli flicked a Liverpool corner into the back of his own net.

With the 'Golden-Goal' rule in effect, the contest was over.

Liverpool were cup-winners for the third time that season. The game had ended 5-4. Not boring at all.

It was an historic cup-treble. One that had never been done before.

Man Utd fans tried to taunt us that ours was a Mickey Mouse treble. The one they had won two years earlier, of Premier League, FA Cup, and Champions League was the more prestigious.

They are right, of course, but ours wasn't bad either. In fact, it was really rather good.

Despite all of this cup success, our season was still not over though. The celebrations would have to wait. The champagne kept on ice.

We had one more league game left to play – an away match at Charlton Athletic.

If we won, we'd qualify for the following season's Champions League in the last available spot. Lose, or even draw, and Leeds United would nip in ahead of us.

Man Utd and Arsenal were already confirmed in the top two places.

Could we raise ourselves for one last effort?

In the first half of the last game of a long and already successful season, it seemed that we could not. Charlton hit the woodwork, had a reasonable penalty appeal turned down, and forced several saves from the Liverpool keeper Sander Westerveld.

Then, in the second half, after what must have been an inspirational team talk from Gerard Houllier, The Reds came out blazing and scored four times: twice from Robbie Fowler, once from Danny Murphy, with the last coming from the prolific, precocious, and prodigious Michael Owen to put the icing on, and cap a fine season.

The youngster finished as our top scorer with 24 goals in all competitions. Heskey came second with a more-than-respectable 22.

Fowler came in third with a not-bad 17.

We had won three cups, and we had Champions League football to look forward to the following season.

The future looked bright.

CHAPTER TWENTY-FIVE

Robbie Fowler was to be a surprise departure in the season. He had found himself at odds with the management team of Gerard Houllier and Phil Thompson after a couple of off-field incidents that saw him hit the front pages of the tabloid press.

As a well-known figure in his home city, he had drawn the wrong sort of attention and bumped into a few supporters of a different football team who let their feelings about him be known.

The first occasion was a late-night drinking session in the Moat House hotel in the centre of town. A couple of lads decided to give him a whack on the nose, and the story somehow hit the papers.

While the dust was still settling on that one, Fowler (who possibly should have known better) went into the city-centre again and made the wrong sort of headlines once more. He seemed to be a magnet for trouble, and the club decided to move him on.

He would be gone before the end of the year, sold to our rivals Leeds United for a significant sum.

Also to leave would be Sander Westerveld and Christian Ziege. Incoming were John-Arne Riise, Milan Baros, and two new goalies in Chris Kirkland and Jerzy Dudek. New faces for a club on the up.

The traditional season opener was the Charity Shield match, which paired the holders of the league title with the winners of the FA Cup.

The former was Man Utd. The latter was us.

In a game again played at the Millennium Stadium, Liverpool raced to a 2-0 lead at half-time. United then pulled one back after the break with a goal from their new signing Ruud Van Nistelrooy.

That was the extent of their comeback and we held on for a 2-1 win.

After the match, Alex Ferguson said that Liverpool would pose a threat to his side in the league in the coming season as they were big and powerful and talented too. No lover of The Reds, Fergie was still a friend and admirer of Gerard Houllier, so his words can be given credence. He meant what he said.

Twelve days later, we were set to face Bayern Munich in the European Super Cup to be played in Monaco. Similar to the Charity Shield format, this one-off match paired the holders of the Champions League with the winners of the UEFA Cup.

Early in the match, Michael Owen sprinted down the right wing before he played in a teasing cross which Riise turned in at the back post for his debut goal.

Then, just before the half-time interval, Heskey scored what was probably the greatest goal of his Liverpool career. It's certainly a favourite of mine.

Heskey took possession of the ball about 30 yards from goal. Seeing no immediate options to pass to a team-mate, he decided to push forward himself, exploiting a gap between the two Bayern Munich central-defenders.

As he sprinted between the pair, they both looked bewildered. How had they left such a gap? These were experienced, professional footballers. This was a move straight out of the schoolyard.

They then turned and attempted to go with him. To no avail.

You know if you ever watch a boat race, say at the Olympics, how one boat goes first, then the other seems to overtake them, with the to-and-fro dictated by the timing of their strokes? It always looks like they are neck and neck, alternating the lead, up until the point where one boat goes forward and then the other, on their stroke, fails to overtake the other boat.

That's when you know who is in front. Your go doesn't match my go.

Well, Heskey sprinted through the gap, and the two defenders turned.

He pushed the ball further forward again, and the Bayern players trailed in his wake.

He simply left them for dead. Bewildered. Befuddled. Bemused.

The German international goalkeeper Oliver Kahn, a colossus of the game, came rushing out and dived at Emile's feet to smother the danger.

Our big centre-forward dinked a dainty little chip over the advancing keeper and into the net. The ball rolled into an empty goal. All opposition had been nullified. It was spontaneous and sublime. A fabulous goal.

Heskey appeared to have surprised himself, as if he didn't know he had it in him.

Michael Owen, following up to share the celebration, approached Heskey with his arms aloft, seeking an embrace. The look on Owen's face said it all.

'Come here, my son. That deserves a hug.'

I know that England fans never really 'got' Heskey. I don't know how many Liverpool fans did either. Houllier did. Phil Thompson did. And I bet if you asked Michael Owen, he'd eulogise till the cows came home.

Two minutes into the second half in the Super Cup final, Owen grabbed one for himself. Liverpool were now 3-0 up against the Champions of Europe.

Despite two late goals from Bayern Munich, we held on for the win.

Added to the three cups from the previous season, plus the Charity Shield and now the Super Cup, we had won five trophies in the last six months.

When the new league season kicked off, hopes amongst supporters were unsurprisingly high. Could we sustain our undoubted ability over the course of a full campaign?

Our first match was at home to West Ham. Owen scored twice in a 2-1 win.

Next up was an away trip to Bolton Wanderers, who were newly-promoted from the division below.

The game was played on Monday the 27th of August. It was an evening kick-off.

The last Monday in August is always an English Bank Holiday. It has always been my favourite day of the year.

In Liverpool, we had the Matthew Street Festival and Beatles Week. Bank Holiday Monday marked the end of festivities. Tribute bands from across the globe would come to play in bars and clubs in the city centre. There would be lots of outdoor stages where you could watch Abba bands, Rod Stewart look-a-likes, and versions of Queen, The Kinks, The Rolling Stones, and loads of others.

It was a feast of music. The streets would be packed. It was nothing short of a carnival.

I would walk into town, as I lived nearby, and meet up with friends and family who loved the day too. My mum would bring a packed lunch. We'd get a carry-out from the off-license and find a spot in front of one of the stages and eat and drink and dance and sing along.

Later on, when the sun went down, we might go into a bar and find a live band on and the revelry would continue.

In 2001, as we had a night match scheduled on this particular Bank Holiday Monday, we ended our day at the festival early and went our separate ways. My family took the train back to other parts of the city, while I made the uphill walk back towards the Georgian quarter of Liverpool 8.

The local pub where I drank did not show the football, so I decided to pop into one of the student bars close to home where I knew they would have the match on.

I was well-oiled by this time. I'd been drinking since about 12 o'clock lunchtime, and it was now eight in the evening.

I found an empty chair at a table occupied by a group of students and plonked myself down.

In good spirits, from the joy of the festival of music and our recent fifth cup win, I eulogised about my magnificent team to the people at the table.

'Bayern Munich,' I said (or probably slurred) are the Champions of Europe, and we beat them, so that means that we, Liverpool, are the best team in Europe.'

I then sat there with a stupid grin on my face, believing whole-heartedly in my ill-thought-out argument.

The match kicked off, and Bolton scored first to lead at half-time. Then Heskey equalised after 66 minutes.

The clock was running down when, in the 90th minute, Dean Holdsworth went and scored to give the Wanderers a 2-1 victory.

I'd seen enough. It was time to go. I stood up to leave and said goodbye to the students who'd suffered my company at their table for the past two hours.

With impeccable logic, and a no-doubt parting shot, the one I'd earlier eulogised to said, 'Does that make Bolton the best team in Europe then?'

I had no answer to that.

Clever bastards some of them students!

We then lost our next league game to Aston Villa, before winning three on the bounce against Everton, Tottenham, and Newcastle United, with two of those matches coming away from home.

Next up was a home game against Leeds United. Both teams had title-aspirations for the coming season. This game could prove to be important and even memorable.

It was, but not in the way that anyone had expected.

At the interval, Liverpool trailed by a goal to nil. The goalscorer was Harry Kewell, who would later join The Reds.

Still with us was Robbie Fowler, but his days at the club were now numbered.

He would go on to set up our second-half equaliser for Danny Murphy in a game that eventually finished in a 1-1 draw, but it was events at half-time that would prove pivotal.

Gerard Houllier – watching from the dugout – felt unwell and complained of chest pains to the club doctor Mark Waller.

One of our players was seeking treatment in the medical room when Gerard came calling.

The manager pulled rank and then explained, with what turned out to be huge understatement, 'I think my need is greater than yours.'

Mark Waller carried out a quick assessment and agreed with the boss. He immediately called for an ambulance to take him to the city's Broadgreen Hospital.

From watching on the sidelines, it would be straight into the operating theatre.

It was then touch and go whether Houllier would ever return.

CHAPTER TWENTY-SIX

Gerard Houllier spent 11 hours on the operating table with a dissected aorta; it's one of the most important arteries in the body, serving the human heart directly.

His recovery would be long and slow, and he might be out for up to a year.

Phil Thompson stood in as caretaker manager of the team.

He didn't do too bad, either. He won six and drew once in his first seven league games in charge. At the end of that sequence, in early December, Liverpool were six points clear at the top of the table.

It was a promising start under Thompson, but we won just one of the next seven matches afterwards.

Some surprising business in the transfer market was the arrival of the exciting French forward Nicolas Anelka, who came to us on loan from Paris St-Germain for the remainder of the season.

I don't think any of the fans saw that one coming, but I think we were all delighted to have him.

The first time I saw him play was in the opening game in our defence of the FA Cup, when Birmingham City came to Anfield in early January.

The left-back for the opposition that day was David Burrows, our former player.

Michael Owen and Anelka were up front for The Reds, the first time they'd been paired together from the start of a match.

A long ball was sent upfield, too far for Anelka to reach, and it landed at the feet of Burrows, who pumped it back from where it came.

Anelka kept closing Burrows down, even though the ball was now nowhere near him.

Burrows must have been thinking 'Where is he going? Why's he still coming towards me?'

Then, as Anelka reached the Birmingham full-back, about ten seconds after the ball had gone, the forward stood on Burrow's foot. Hard!

It was just the Frenchman's way of letting the defender know that he was there.

And it worked. Liverpool went on to win by three goals to nil, with Anelka getting the last of the three to cap a fine night's work as he began to forge a formidable strike-partnership with Owen.

The Reds then beat Man Utd at Old Trafford in the league, with Danny Murphy scoring the winner for the second season running. It began a remarkable run of results.

I can recall a fabulous quote from Houllier about Danny Murphy. The manager said that, tactically, Danny was our most important player. We were blessed with an outstanding array of midfielders at the time: Hamann, McAllister, Steven Gerrard, Vladimir Smicer, and Patrick Berger.

What Houllier meant was, he's not our best player, but he's the only one who bleedin' listens to me! Murphy was the only one that would follow instructions to the letter.

We then won 10 of our next 11 matches to move up from fifth place to second in the league. The upturn sparked partly by the return to the dugout of Gerard Houllier, who came back on an emotional European night at home to Roma in the Champions League.

He should have sat out the season, and also taken the summer holidays to recuperate; as pleased as we all were to have him back, he looked frail and fragile after his too-close brush with death.

And while we had given a terrific account of ourselves in our league campaign, we simply could not overhaul Arsenal who would go on to lift the title.

The Reds finished in second place, our highest finish in more than a decade.

We had also reached the quarter-finals of the Champions League before losing to eventual finalists Bayer Leverkusen.

While there were no trophies to show this year, we had given a good account of ourselves. And who knows what might have happened had our manager not fallen ill, missing a big part of the season.

Another disappointment was the decision not to turn Anelka's loan deal into a permanent transfer.

I think his team-mates – as well as the fans – were surprised with that.

Anelka had come with the reputation of being a bit of a sulk. His brothers were acting as his agents, and they were said to be difficult to deal with. This might have been the reason why, despite being just 23 years of age, he'd already had three previous clubs in his career, including Arsenal and Real Madrid, as well as PSG.

Still, Anelka was so keen to sign permanently for Liverpool that he turned up in Gerard Houllier's office without his agent brothers and effectively said that he would sign whatever contract Houllier put in front of him.

I'm sure that – had Gerard not had his heart issues – he would have taken Anelka on. But, not feeling 100% fit, he probably didn't want to work with someone whose moods were unpredictable.

In the close season, Anelka returned to Paris, and Houllier brought in El Hadji Diouf instead.

Sometimes, you can't help thinking about the one that got away.

Hopes were still high after our second-place finish, and we began the following league campaign in fine fashion.

For a season that started in mid-August, it would be November before we would taste our first defeat, having won nine and drawn three of our first dozen matches.

Could we go one better than the season before and finally write our name upon the Premier League trophy?

After our blistering start, we were sitting pretty at the top of the table, four points clear of Arsenal. And then the wheels fell off. There would be no more wins in November. None in December. It was well into the second half of January before we picked up another three points.

Our league campaign was effectively over for another year. Luckily, we again booked our place in a final where we were due to play Man Utd in the League Cup.

Thanks to goals from Steven Gerrard and Michael Owen, Liverpool emerged victorious, and Gerard Houllier confirmed his terrific run of results against Alex Ferguson.

Despite the silverware, the team were on course for a disappointing fifth-placed finish.

Amongst the fans, and in the boardroom, people were starting to wonder if Houllier's Liverpool team had begun to stagnate.

What could he do in the transfer market to bolster our situation? He'd have to do a lot better than in the previous transfer window, as neither Diouf, Salif Diao, or Bruno Cheyrou, his three marquee signings, had set the world alight. Most supporters considered them a waste of money.

Could Houllier do better the next time around? The truth was that *he had to*; otherwise, his time at the club would soon be up.

For the 2003/2004 season, Houllier brought in two French youngsters in Anthony le Tallec and Florent Sinama Pongolle, calling them his 'gems'. He also captured the signature of Harry Kewell from Leeds United.

Out went Patrick Berger.

We still had Michael Owen banging the goals in, but there was clearly a rift between him and the fans. I don't think Owen deserved this. All he had ever done was give his all for us.

I remember I was employed in a surveyor's office in Liverpool at the time. We had a year-out student working with us. He was a Man Utd supporter.

He was telling me one day how lucky we were to have a goalscorer of Owen's quality. I told him that I hadn't heard Owen's name chanted at the match for over three years.

Christian, the student, was astounded.

'I thought you all loved him,' he said.

'I do,' I replied, 'but no-one else seems to.'

I believe Owen was so confused by it all that he even asked his good friend and team-mate Jamie Carragher about it. Words to the effect of 'What have I done wrong?'

The answer was 'nothing', but once an idea takes hold (which in this case was that Owen cared more about playing for his country than he did for Liverpool), then it's a difficult task to change people's minds.

Unfortunately, apart from the FA Cup final, where no-one could deny that he had won it for us, I don't think Owen ever got the adoration that his talent and goals for the club deserved.

Come the time of Owen's departure, he wasn't the only one that the supporters appeared to have fallen out of love with.

Our manager, Gerard Houllier, was also not in many fans' best-books.

My dad has a mate called Jack Austin. He is a great reader of the game. He had previously played semi-pro football for Skelmersdale United in the same team as former Reds-legend Stevie Heighway. Jack could both talk and play a great game.

I was still in Houllier's camp. Many people weren't. Jack amongst them. He felt the manager had peaked with that cup-treble and was now going backwards.

The new season would tell us if that was really true. I hoped it wasn't.

We then didn't get off to the best of starts, losing 2-1 at home to Chelsea before two scoreless draws in our next two games.

We won our next three matches, and then lost the next three on the bounce.

With half the season gone, our best league position had been fifth, while our average placing was a lot lower than that.

We'd not fared well in the cup competitions either.

Despite a slight improvement in the second half of the season, we eventually finished in fourth place. We couldn't lay a glove on leaders Arsenal. That said, neither could anyone else in what was to be their 'Invincibles' season when The Gunners went through the entire campaign undefeated on their way to lifting the Premier League.

Houllier had one year remaining on his contract when the season came to a close.

He'd previously won five cups in six months before he was stopped in his tracks by major heart issues.

Though he had rushed back early to try and help the team, he had probably come back too soon.

I wondered what we might have won had his health issues not appeared when they did. I was sure we were on a winning trajectory.

Apart from his decision not to sign Anelka, he had done little wrong in my eyes.

The club, however, saw it differently.

He was asked to resign with 12 months still remaining on the contract he had signed.

I was disappointed. Not just because I believed in him, but also from a moral standpoint.

We weren't a sacking club. In our 112-year history, we had only sent two men, Don Welsh and Graeme Souness, packing.

Now it had happened to Houllier, who had won the League Cup just the season before and who had, prior to his heart problems, delivered us our finest trophy-winning period since the glory days of the 1970s and 1980s.

I thought he should have been allowed to see out his contract. Maybe he'd have got us back on track. Maybe not. We'll never know. He deserved better than having the rug pulled from under him, but he left with the well-wishes of many of the fans.

Gary McAllister summed up Gerard's time at Anfield by saying he thought the team needed to play with a bit more freedom if they were ever going to win the Premiership. Our set-up was made for cup competitions. We had a counter-attacking style of play that could win us matches, but we needed to open up a bit if we were going to win the league. You have to have the attitude, McAllister said, that if the opposition score two, we'll score three. That's the outlook that wins titles.

There spoke the voice of experience. It was advice that every Liverpool fan hoped our next manager would heed.

It was 'Au revoir' Gerard Houllier, and 'Hola' Rafa Benitez.

CHAPTER TWENTY-SEVEN

In 2004, Valencia won the Spanish League and the UEFA Cup. Their manager, Rafa Benitez, was voted by UEFA as the best manager in Europe.

With Gerard Houllier gone, Benitez was an obvious choice to succeed him. Rafa had broken the hegemony of Real Madrid and Barcelona in Spain, winning La Liga twice in the previous three years.

Could he do the same for us? We needed to squeeze past Arsenal and Man United, and Chelsea who, with owner Roman Abramovich's millions, and new manager Jose Mourinho, were the new kids on the block and a team going places.

Mourinho had also expressed interest in the vacant Liverpool manager's job. He had just won the Champion's League with Porto.

The club opted for Benitez instead. The snub may have played a part in what subsequently became animosity. Or maybe Mourinho just wanted to crush everyone anyway.

It certainly seemed that way; Pep Guardiola later labelled him an 'enemy of football'.

So Rafa Benitez became our new manager.

League results would be up and down.

Transfer activity would be interesting.

Djibril Cisse came in for a fee of £14.5 million. We also bought in Xabi Alonso and Luis Garcia, both of whom became firm crowd-favourites.

We lost Michael Owen to Real Madrid for a ridiculously-low £8.5 million. That number should have had a three, four, or even a five in front of it.

I guess Owen just got bored of doing the business week-in and week-out, season after season, for little appreciation from the stands.

It was time to move on.

Now a new manager might be expected to take a little time to get used to a new league, a new country, and opposition of whom he had little understanding.

That certainly appeared to be the case as we lost a staggering 14 of our 38 Premier League games in Rafa's first campaign in charge.

At one point, we were lower than our cross-city rivals Everton in the league standings. The Toffees started calling him Rafa Beneath-us! You had to laugh.

We also went out of the FA Cup at the first attempt.

Benitez did manage to take us to the League Cup final in February, where we lost to Chelsea by three goals to two. The deciding strike was actually an own-goal by Steven Gerrard.

Jose Mourinho was trying to attract Gerrard to Chelsea at the time, singing his praises, and the Liverpool midfielder did little to bat away their interest. It looked like he might leave us and join our rivals.

After that headed own-goal in the final, the joke went around Chelsea fans that 'He hasn't even joined us yet and he's scored his first goal for us!'

The prospect of losing what was undoubtedly the club's best player did not make Benitez's first season in charge any easier.

But the real hope, and the manager's real experience, lay in Europe.

And there, we were about to make history.

Entering the competition at the third-round qualifying stage, we overcame a two-legged tie against unknown Grazer AK of Austria and proceeded to the first group stage alongside Monaco, Olympiacos, and Deportivo La Coruna.

Results in the Champions League were mixed, literally, with a win, a draw, and a defeat in our first three matches.

We then beat Coruna and lost to Monaco, which meant that we had to beat Olympiacos by two clear goals in our final group game to progress to the knockout stages.

I was studying at the time for my MA in Writing. The course took place every Wednesday evening between six and nine pm in the shadow of the Anglican Cathedral in the heart of Liverpool.

I made it to a pub across the road just in time to catch the second half. I met some friends there and asked how we were doing. 'Not good' was their response.

We were trailing by a goal to nil and needed to score three to win.

Sinama Pongolle came on as a substitute at the interval, and made an immediate impression as he bundled the ball across the goal-line to get us back in the match.

The game was edging towards a nervy last ten minutes, with the scores still tied, when another Benitez substitution, this time in Neil Mellor, again brought instant dividends.

Liverpool were in front, but we still weren't out of the woods; we needed another goal to progress.

Then, with four minutes of normal time left, Steven Gerrard struck a powerful shot into the back of the net at the Kop end of the ground.

We were through to the next round of the Champions League! Our journey-proper had begun.

Bayer Leverkusen were our opponents in the first knockout stage. We managed to beat them 3-1 both home and away, with our new winger Luis Garcia scoring once in the first game and twice in the return leg.

Next up were the Italian giants Juventus.

A rare Sami Hyypia volley put The Reds in front, and then a wonderful half-volley from Luis Garcia sent the Anfield crowd into ecstasy. It was one of those 'I was there' moments and 'I was there' goals.

Fabio Cannavaro then pulled one back for the visitors to make for a tense last 30 minutes, but we held on to take a slender victory back to Turin for the away leg.

We had a makeshift team at the time. Benitez was having to think on his feet. The list of players available for selection seemed to change every week. It was no easy task to pick a strong starting XI, never mind to then be able to pick a strong bench.

Our first-choice goalie, Jerzy Dudek, had missed the first leg through injury. He came back into the team for the return fixture, replacing 19-year-old Scott Carson who kept goal for the first leg of the tie.

In, too, came Xabi Alonso, making his first start for three months. He would take the place of Steven Gerrard, who was another recent addition to our ever-growing injury list.

On the bench was Djibril Cisse, who had been out for more than six months of his debut season, having suffered a broken leg in a league game against Blackburn.

It was a patched-up team that had the responsibility of preserving our well-earned lead, and our place in the competition. With so many players returning from injury and therefore short of match-practice, resilience would be needed, as the Italians were bound to come out fighting.

Despite Juventus twice hitting the post, a well-organised Liverpool side held on for the draw to take our place in the semi-final.

Our opponents in the tie would be Chelsea. Their manager Jose Mourinho was enjoying a very successful first season in charge of the London club. He had arrived as a Champions League-winning manager with Porto, and was on his way to winning the Premier League to go with the League Cup he had already wrapped up, at our expense, earlier that year.

It seemed that the Special One could do no wrong. He had the winning touch. How was anyone going to stop them?

The first of the two ties was held at Stamford Bridge. There were chances for both sides, but Liverpool managed to hold on for a 0-0 draw to give us an opportunity to progress at Anfield in front of our own fans.

The night's only disappointment, apart from not securing a valuable away goal, was a harsh yellow card for Xabi Alonso that meant he would miss the return fixture.

As we were already at full-stretch, going from game to game plugging the gaps as best we could, this wouldn't make the second leg task any easier.

The booking for Alonso was particularly galling as Eidur Gudjohnsen appeared to taunt him in the aftermath. Alonso had only just returned to the side after having had his ankle broken following an unpleasant tackle by Frank Lampard in an earlier league fixture between the two teams.

Lampard was only one yellow card away from a one-match suspension himself. I think Mourinho told him to get one in that game, which meant he would miss an easy FA Cup tie but would then be available for the rest of the league campaign that was going so well for them.

Frank lunged in, a little too forcefully on Xabi, breaking his ankle.

Told in the post-match interview by a knowing reporter that he had earned the right to miss a comfortable FA Cup game as a result of the suspension, (i.e. there were dark works in play), Lampard did his best to keep a straight face, feigning all-knowledge. He took Mourinho's instructions as read, went in too hard, and seriously injured Alonso. A professional foul it was. Professional sportsmanship it was not.

Our silky Spanish midfielder would be a big miss for the second leg of the tie.

With Chelsea flying in the league, it was already a big ask to try to knock Mourinho's team out of their stride.

Well, it seemed that Benitez had a plan to do just that.

He told a bemused press conference, the night before the big game, that Liverpool would win.

When one reporter pointed out that Chelsea were a magnificent side and, at the time, apparently an unstoppable force, Rafa merely repeated that Chelsea were a great side, but that we would win.

There was no hiding place from that. Lose, and he would look like an idiot. Win, and he would look like a sage.

And Benitez's plan?

To get at Chelsea early, to come flying out of the blocks and attack them from the kick-off, to use the sound and fury of the fans to overwhelm the Londoners in those first few minutes, before they knew what had hit them.

And it worked.

Luis Garcia scrambled the ball over the Chelsea goal-line.

A flick from Steven Gerrard sent Milan Baros free in the box. About to score, he got wiped out by the onrushing Chelsea keeper Petr Cech.

As Baros appealed, rightly, for a penalty, Garcia followed up and tapped the ball goalwards.

While Chelsea attempted to clear the goal-bound shot, the referee deemed the ball to have already crossed the line. Garcia had already peeled away in celebration, which may give some clue as to whether it had actually gone in or not.

Liverpool then rode their luck, Eidur Gudjohnsen coming particularly close, and held on in there for a famous win.

Mourinho called Garcia's strike a 'ghost goal'.

Whatever.

I'd have taken the penalty and the sending off for Cech. With 86 minutes left to play, we would probably have gone on to beat a ten-man Chelsea team far more convincingly than we ultimately did.

The result meant that it would be The Reds who progressed to the Champions League final. It would be us on the pitch in Istanbul.

It would be our name writing history, for history we certainly did write.

Football games did not come more dramatic than this. We were about to witness something extraordinary on a night that Liverpool fans will never forget.

CHAPTER TWENTY-EIGHT

Films have been made about that night at the Ataturk Stadium in Istanbul. Plays have been written. Stories have been told and re-told, and will continue to be expressed for the next 100 years. Here's mine.

Forget trying to get a ticket for the final. They were like gold-dust.

I used to play five-a-side football every week. After the game, we used to go for a drink in a student bar behind the Everyman Theatre in the city centre.

As we were loyal customers, keeping them going during the summer months when their usual clientele had gone home, the manager offered to reserve a table for us right in front of the big screen. Of course, we said yes.

A mate from work asked me where I was going to watch the match.

I told him the venue we had chosen.

'A student bar!' he said, clearly unimpressed by my response. 'How is that going to have any atmosphere for our biggest game in years?'

My colleague and me, along with about eight others from the footy, went and took our places at our specially-reserved table.

They were the best seats in the house, and drew envious glances from others in the room.

On the pitch, Liverpool were definitely the underdogs, despite our rich heritage in the competition.

We had won it on four previous occasions, a record for an English club.

A fifth win and the trophy, that magnificent pot of silverware affectionately known as 'Big Ears', would be ours to keep forever.

AC Milan, though, were firm favourites on the night.

Our own forward line-up consisted of Harry Kewell, at times mercurial and at others mediocre, alongside the young Czech player Milan Baros. Djibril Cisse was on the bench.

They weren't bad, those three, but Owen and Heskey, backed up by Robbie Fowler, they certainly were not.

In the opposition camp, AC Milan could boast Andriy Shevchenko and Hernan Crespo up front, two of the best centre-forwards in the world.

The rest of their team was outstanding too.

Three-quarters of the stadium, three sides of the ground, were filled with Liverpool fans. We always went with massive support for these European games, as if to confirm our standing on the continent.

Back at home, the city of Liverpool was heaving. It was standing room only in most of the bars.

Except for us, of course, with our well-positioned table right in front of the large TV screen.

Nerves were jangling. Beer was bought. The clock ticked down to kick-off.

In the dressing room before the game, Benitez told the team to play it long if we won the toss. Show Milan that we intended to attack them. It would be a statement of intent. Aim for Baros. Put them on the back foot immediately.

The game kicked off. We played it short, conceded a free-kick, and Paolo Maldini hooked the ball into the Liverpool net. We were a goal behind in the Champions League final with less than a minute on the clock.

The misery would be confounded with two further goals, both coming from Hernan Crespo, before the half-time interval.

Benitez then made a tactical change, bringing on Didi Hamann for defender Steve Finnan to try to stop us getting overrun in midfield. It had been happening for much of the first 45 minutes.

Nine minutes after the restart, Steven Gerrard rose above several Milan defenders to power in a header and begin the fightback of all fightbacks.

Vladimir Smicer then struck a second in what would turn out to be his last ever game for The Reds.

Some players might switch off a little when they know that their contract is about to run out. Benitez, showing a certain psychological nous, had emphasised to the players who would soon be moving on that they shouldn't take their foot off the gas just yet.

He'd urged them to think of the different offers they might receive, and their increased bargaining power when it came to signing-on fees and wages, if they went to their new employers as Champions League winners. It worked a treat.

And then there were the fans. A rousing chorus of our anthem 'You'll never walk alone' had greeted the team as they returned to the pitch for round two of what was proving to be a bruising encounter.

With Steven Gerrard dragging the team forward, and Hamann having a positive influence in a midfield holding role, Liverpool had got themselves back into the game.

AC Milan were rattled, sensing they might be on the verge of throwing away a winning position and inviting humiliation onto themselves.

The pressure soon told on the Italian team and, when Gerrard went down in the box after a determined forward run, Xabi Alonso stepped up to take the resulting penalty.

Despite his first attempt being saved by their Brazilian goalkeeper, Dida, Alonso fired the rebound into the roof of the net.

The comeback was complete, for now. We had turned our fortunes around.

In the student bar, I was by now up on the table, as were many others, dancing with joy.

The whole place was bouncing. Everyone was hugging everybody else.

Delirium and happiness was written all over our faces.

I turned to Chris from work and asked him 'Is this enough atmosphere for you?'

It was, but there was still the remainder of the game, and then extra-time, and ultimately a penalty shootout to negotiate.

It was 3-3 at the end of 90 minutes.

In the additional 30 minutes of play, AC Milan were dominant, trying to put right and make amends for what they'd let slip from their grasp.

With three minutes of open play remaining, Shevchenko headed an inviting cross downwards towards the bottom corner of Dudek's goal.

The keeper got a hand to it, but Shevchenko was following up with intent.

From no more than two yards out, he put his boot through the ball.

He thought he had scored. Was certain to score. There could be no mistake.

Dudek was lying prone on the ground but, with the most superb of reflexes, he stuck up a hand and diverted a pinpoint, powerful shot, up and over the cross-bar.

I've never seen anything like it. Shevchenko was astounded.

It was a spectacular double save, and served to deflate Milan even more than they already were. It seemed to say to the Italians 'Sorry boys, this ain't your night'.

And then came the penalty shootout.

Jamie Carragher had reminded Dudek of Bruce Grobbelaar's antics in the 1984 European Cup final. The wobbly-legs routine had put the opposition off that time. Could it work again?

It did. Serginho and Andrea Pirlo both missed the first two attempts for Milan, while Hamann and Cisse both scored for The Reds.

AC Milan then scored their next one, while Riise missed for us.

When Kaka slotted for the opposition, it meant we were two-all from the penalty spot, but Liverpool still had a shot in hand.

Smicer then stepped up to score his second of the game, and Shevchenko had to score for the Italians to keep the tie alive.

No doubt jinxed by all that had happened in the match, the Ukrainian centre-forward fluffed his lines once more, sending a weak shot down the middle of the goal, which Dudek comfortably saved with one hand.

The Liverpool players went crazy, running across the pitch to celebrate with the keeper.

Twenty minutes later, the scenes of Steven Gerrard lifting that magnificent trophy will live long in the memory of all Reds' supporters.

There was disbelief, pandemonium, and pure and unadulterated ecstasy for all of our fans, for those in the stadium, those watching at home, and everywhere across the globe.

I didn't even wish I was there at the Ataturk. To be in the centre of Liverpool that night was simply phenomenal.

My friends and I moved to another bar even closer to the action. I saw some sort of Jeep, on 'big-truck' wheels, driving down the street, sirens blazing. It was obviously only given an airing on the most special of occasions. This was one of them.

Horns were honked, songs were sung, and beers were drunk in abundance.

It was a celebration. It was a relief. It was a fifth winning of the European Cup which meant that the trophy belonged to us. Forever.

The following day, while many bleary-eyed Scousers were still making their way back from Istanbul, we had a homecoming parade to look forward to.

I lived in a ground floor flat just a mile from the city centre.

There were about 12 of us sat drinking and watching events unfold on TV.

Some people had been stood in the centre of town for hours and hours, waiting for the team bus to arrive.

We watched the procession until we could see them getting close to the finish line outside of St George's Hall. Then we walked into town.

There were at least a hundred thousand people lined up in front of one of Liverpool's finest and most iconic buildings.

Supporters stood on the roofs of adjacent properties and businesses, and clambered up lampposts and traffic lights. Anything to get a good vantage point.

I was in amongst the crowd, there with a group of mates. I knew, from having watched events unfold on local TV, that it wouldn't be long before the team and the trophy appeared.

I looked at the huge mass of spectators.

Honestly, I thought to myself, all of this is just because we've won a cup.

Was it really all worth it?

Then, the team-bus came into view.

There was our captain, Steven Gerrard, stood front and centre holding aloft the cup of our dreams.

And I immediately got it.

This was no ordinary piece of silverware. It was huge, gleaming, and spectacular.

I thought I was gazing at the Holy Grail itself!

From being a sceptic just a few seconds earlier, I was now almost on my knees, struck down in awe at the sheer spectacle of this magnificent object, of all that the trophy symbolised, and of the journey we had taken to win it.

It was an incredible moment. One that I will never forget.

All of the effort, facing down and overcoming our opponents, even riding our luck – had all been for this.

Victory in Istanbul had been an unbelievable end to Rafa's first year in charge.

Could this man, who had delivered our fifth European Cup, also be our saviour in the Premier League?

When our hangovers had dissipated, we would soon find out, as we got ready – as the Champions of Europe – to face another season.

No one would have dreamt of such a thing just 12 months before.

I can remember when Rafa first took over as our manager. I watched him in his first game in charge.

Liverpool scored a goal, and instead of celebrating, Rafa merely grabbed his notebook and made a few further pointers to the players.

There was no 'Wow, we scored. I can really work at this level.' It was just business, purely business. He was totally focussed on the next move, the next goal, the next win.

He'd had the same focus when working as the manager of Real Madrid's B team when he was a young coach. His own father came to watch him one night to lend him some support. At the end of the game, Rafa walked right past him, not even noticing him, still writing in his notebook.

His father rightly remonstrated with him afterwards. 'You might be the manager of Real's B-team... but I'm still your father.'

Rafa apologised. He'd meant nothing by it. He'd simply been so wrapped up in the job at hand that he had no periphery. Only focus. And ambition.

We'd need some of that dedication going forward but, to summarise season one of the Rafa revolution, we'd had the most incredible and fabulous start.

CHAPTER TWENTY-NINE

We were champions of Europe, back in the big bed. We had surprised everyone, including ourselves, and were now a familiar name once more amongst the elite.

Rafa Benitez knew that he had gotten as much as he could out of the squad and the players that he had. He also knew that the fans craved a Premier League title.

Within 36 hours of that emotional cup-final victory, Rafa was back at his desk at our Melwood training facility, plotting his way forward for the coming campaign.

Which players would go? Who would come in? What contracts did he need to negotiate or renegotiate?

He knew that we needed to strengthen to mount a challenge in the league. In came Peter Crouch and Mohamed Sissoko, Boudewijn Zenden, and a new goalkeeper in Pepe Reina.

Despite Dudek's heroics in Istanbul, he was not the answer to the question between the sticks. He was either fantastic or error-prone. The defence needed to know where they stood.

Reina came in for a sizeable sum and, in the years to come, would prove to be money well-spent.

Out went Milan Baros, Igor Biscan, and El Hadji-Diouf.

An early upset involved an announcement from Steven Gerrard that he had decided to leave Liverpool. It sent shock-waves through the club, the city, and supporters across the world.

Chelsea had lodged a bid of £32 million. Steven wanted to go.

Rafa, the chairman David Moores, and our Chief Executive Rick Parry, all tried to talk him out of the move.

They explained their ambition for the club, how important Gerrard was to that blueprint, and asked him to at least take the night to think about it, discuss it with his family, and sleep on it.

He did, and by the following morning, he announced a U-turn and his decision was reversed.

The thought of losing our best player did not bear thinking about. He had been a revelation since he first broke into the side in 1998. He had played right-back then and, despite some stiff competition for that position, made it his own. When he played in midfield, he more than held his own with our best players there. In one game, I saw him cover at left-back. He was the best left-back we had all season. It seemed like there was nothing that he could not do. We were all just so glad he decided to stay.

Gerrard signed a new and improved contract, and Rafa's preparations for the forthcoming season could resume.

Things did not start well, though. We had won one and drawn four of our first five league games before we suffered a humiliating 4-1defeat to Gerrard-fanciers, Chelsea, at Anfield.

We then recovered to win 11 of our next 12 matches to end the calendar year in third place in the league.

In the second half of the season, we won 13, drew three, and lost just four of our last 20 matches.

We finished with a tally of 82 points, behind league-winners Chelsea, and runners-up Man Utd.

It was a respectable total. We had won every one of our last nine games. We were becoming contenders, but others were still ahead of us.

We did, however, have the consolation of an FA Cup final against West Ham.

Could we be cup kings again? Did Rafa really have the golden touch?

It seemed that he might when we set foot at what was proving to be a happy hunting ground for us, the Millennium Stadium in Cardiff.

It would not be an easy game, but it would be memorable in so many ways.

I'd gone to watch it in the same student bar where I'd watched the miracle of Istanbul. It was becoming a lucky boozer, just as this Welsh stadium was turning out to be.

Exactly *how* lucky was made apparent when my mate and I turned up about five minutes before the kick-off.

The pub was rammed.

We stood there, newly-bought pints in hand, wondering where we might best position ourselves to catch a glimpse of the TV and not be standing in anyone else's way.

Two female students were sat on a sofa directly in front of the largest screen in the place.

They were finishing off their drinks and appeared to be packing up.

'Are you leaving?' I asked.

'Yes,' they replied.

They had no interest in the football and were heading home before the match started.

My mate Ashley and I jumped into the empty seats before anyone else could nab them. It could not have worked out better.

Meanwhile, on the pitch, things weren't going quite so well. West Ham were the underdogs, but apparently no-one had informed them of this.

With just 28 minutes on the clock, The Hammers were 2-0 up.

Liverpool then pulled one back through Cisse, and survived a series of scares to scrape through to half-time nursing just the one-goal deficit.

Early in the second half, Steven Gerrard scored to level the game, before a lofted ball from Konchesky, intended as a cross, flew over Pepe Reina's head and into the back of the net.

As the clock ticked down towards the end of the game, it did not look like it was going to be our day.

Then, in the 90th minute, in what could have been our last attack, we sent a hopeful ball forward, which West Ham cleared. It bounced out towards our captain, Gerrard, who struck it right-footed on the half-volley from 35 yards out.

It flew like a missile into the bottom corner of the net, past a startled Shaka Hislop's outstretched hand.

It was a wonderful goal. I think it's the best one Stevie scored in his whole career, which is some statement.

It levelled the scores, and the final would go to extra-time, and then onto a penalty shoot-out.

It was now Pepe Reina's turn to play the hero. He saved three of the West Ham penalties to see Liverpool lift the cup.

There was no league title to crow about, but Rafa's reign had produced two major trophies in his first two seasons in charge.

Our points tally in the league was also our highest since the 1980s.

It seemed to indicate that improvement had been made.

Come the next season, could we go all the way?

We would find out after the summer when the new campaign started, but there was the small matter of the World Cup to get out of the way first.

It would be held in Germany, and I would be there together with the five-a-side lads.

One of our group had a nephew who was a golf pro at a course just outside of Stuttgart. He had secured us a four-bed, eight-berth chalet next to the course, and the use of a minibus for the week.

There were eight of us there, and we spent the whole seven days watching football, either at matches or the fan park in Stuttgart surrounded by beer tents, supporters of every nation, and beautiful women.

The sun was shining. Holidays didn't get much better than this.

We drove to Munich one day and went to the magnificent Allianz Arena to watch the Ivory Coast beat Serbia and Montenegro by three goals to two.

The England national team, meanwhile, progressed from their group and then beat Ecuador to set up a quarter-final tie against Portugal.

The game ended 0-0 and eventually went to penalties where (surprise, surprise), England lost.

Gerrard and Carragher both missed their punts in the shoot-out.

England would be coming home.

So were we.

It was one of those weeks where I would happily have turned the clock back and done it all again.

It was back to domesticity and the domestic league season.

How was Rafa going to cap his previous good work? We appeared to be closing the gap on the clubs above us, but they still seemed tantalisingly out of reach.

Perhaps our new signings would help.

Craig Bellamy was one of them: a fast and feisty centre-forward, and a constant irritant to opposition defenders (and opposition fans), but a great player to have on your side.

We also brought in Jermaine Pennant, a tricky winger, from Birmingham, as well as Dirk Kuyt, an honest and energetic striker from Holland.

Benitez had obviously identified the front line as an area of the squad that needed strengthening. We had spent over £20 million on forward players alone. We had silverware in the trophy cabinet, and confidence out on the pitch.

Would 2006/2007 see us win that elusive league?

Benitez knew how much it meant to the club and the fans.

He would give it his best shot.

CHAPTER THIRTY

The 2006/2007 season started with a trip to Bramall Lane and a 1-1 draw against Sheffield United.

Our goalscorer that day, from the penalty spot, was our old friend Robbie Fowler, who had rejoined the club on a free transfer from Manchester City (who he had previously joined from Leeds) towards the end of the previous campaign.

Victory in our next game, at home to West Ham, was followed by an embarrassing 3-0 loss to our city-rivals Everton.

This was exacerbated by defeat in our next match at Stamford Bridge away to Chelsea. Winners of the league title last time around, they were proving that they would be no pushovers this time either.

We stuttered through the rest of September, and it was the same story right through October.

November brought just two wins from five matches.

It seemed that our new signings and our constantly changing squad were taking time to settle in and gel as a team.

December brought much better results with five wins from six. We moved up to third place in the league, and would more or less stay there for the remainder of the season.

January saw us exit both the League Cup and the FA Cup, twice at the hands of Arsenal.

In the League Cup game, we lost by six goals to three. At home! It was the first time anyone had scored that many goals against us, at Anfield, in almost 80 years.

I was there that night. Cesc Fabregas pulled all the strings for The Gunners. Our weakened team, with Benitez resting many of his first-choice players, just could not cope with Arsenal's brilliant young Spanish midfielder. Or with Julio Baptista who scored four of Arsenal's goals. No wonder that his nickname was 'The Beast'.

I'd been working in Sheffield that week. My car was an old jalopy. My dad said he had two tickets available if I could make it back in time.

The motorway traffic was horrendous, and got worse the closer I got to Liverpool. There was snow on the ground.

I had to go and collect my mate in Toxteth who was taking the second ticket. I didn't think I'd make it, but I escaped the traffic, negotiated the back roads, picked my mate up, and drove to Anfield.

My dad had left our tickets behind the bar of a pub where he drank before the game. We had only missed the first five minutes when we took our seats, and the score was still 0-0. Little did we realise the drama to come.

While the result was disappointing, and the first time anyone had scored six against us at Anfield since 1930, I still felt kind of glad that I was there. It was a result that comes along once in a lifetime. And I was there to see it, as hard as it was to watch.

But it wasn't all bad news in the cup competitions.

We had progressed beyond the group stage in the Champions League, and had been drawn against the might of Barcelona in the first knockout round.

The Spaniards were the current holders of the cup. We'd won the competition the year before that, so it was a match between the two most recent winners.

The game was scheduled for the back end of February. It was going to be an interesting contest but, off the field at Anfield, things were getting interesting too.

David Moores, the Liverpool chairman, had decided that he could not compete with the new breed of owner being drawn to the world of football. Their finances simply dwarfed his own, and he feared that the club he loved would be left behind.

He could not fund the improvements that were needed to both the squad and the Anfield stadium.

One of the people interested in buying the club was Sheikh Mohammed Mansour, whose personal wealth had been put at £17 billion. His family as a whole were worth somewhere in the region of £1 trillion!

Instead of shaking hands with the Sheikh, Moores opted to sell his 51% stake in the club to two Americans, Tom Hicks and George Gillett, who arrived with big promises.

Like most Texans, they could certainly talk the talk.

It wasn't long before the Liverpool fans and their manager wished that they would also walk the walk. Preferably as far away from Anfield as possible.

The promised investment failed to materialise. Conversely, the interest on the loans they had taken out to buy the club started to impact on the manager's plans for the team.

It wasn't long before Liverpool supporters realised how poor – in every sense of the word – our new owners were when the toxic truth began to emerge.

It turned out they were only in it for the money. Go figure! What was the world coming to? But all of that mayhem, madness, and meltdown that was to come was still a couple of years in the future.

First, we had to deal with Barcelona at the Nou Camp.

Benitez took the team to Portugal the week before the big match, both to relax and prepare, and to get in some warm-weather training.

One night, the players all went out for a few drinks at a bar in the Algarve called Monty's.

They had a karaoke machine there, and the team were all encouraging each other to join in.

John Arne Riise refused to take part. Craig Bellamy called him out for it. Cross-words were spoken. Very cross-words, apparently.

The reported line from the fiery little Welshman was 'I'll f*cking do you!' A threat that he later made good on.

The argument between the pair simmered for the rest of the evening and then continued on the minibus back to the hotel.

There, Bellamy went up to his room and returned with a golf club, which he wrapped around Riise's leg!

It was not ideal preparation for a match against Barcelona. How were we going to beat them at the Nou Camp? How were we going to beat them when we were fighting amongst ourselves?

They had Messi, Xavi, Deco, Puyol, Motta, Iniesta, Saviola, and Ronaldhino. We had Finnan, Carragher, Agger, and Arbeloa trying to keep them out.

Barcelona were considered the best team in the world at that time.

With 14 minutes gone in the game, it looked like we would fall victim to their superiority, like so many others had done, when the artful Deco sent a bullet-header past Pepe Reina.

Straight afterwards, the Catalan club had two further gilt-edged chances to cement their lead, but failed to increase the goal margin.

Then, with two minutes to go until half-time, and with Liverpool seemingly holding on for dear life, Steve Finnan sprinted up the right wing and sent in an inviting cross which Bellamy headed home.

How to celebrate a goal against Barcelona at the Nou Camp? With a golf swing of course, and that's what Bellamy did.

I believe one of the big bookmakers was offering decent odds on Bellamy scoring and then doing just that. I don't think anyone thought he'd be so crass, or so cheeky, but it turned out that he was!

Then, with just 16 minutes of the 90 remaining, Bellamy turned provider as he set up – you've guessed it – John Arne Riise to score the winner.

No English team had beaten Barcelona on their home ground in the previous 41 meetings. The last to do so was, err, Liverpool, back in 1976.

We held on for a historic victory. We were halfway there.

We just had to get through the return leg at Anfield.

Although we would go on to lose that game by a goal to nil, we still went through to the next round on the European away-goals rule.

Watching in the stands that night were the new owners, Hicks and Gillett.

Knowing little to nothing about football, the Americans must have been extremely confused to find the Kop and all of the Liverpool supporters celebrating wildly, when we had lost the match!

I can imagine them sitting up in the director's box, like Statler and Waldorf from The Muppets.

'Hey, didn't we just get beat?'

'I think so.'

'Then why is everybody cheering and looking so happy?'

'Beats me!'

I'm sure someone told them the score in the end.

We were through to the quarter-finals of the Champions League.

We were drawn against PSV Eindhoven of Holland.

As a kid, I used to go to Holland every summer as both my dad's sister and my dad's brother, together with their families, had moved there.

They lived in a little place called Papendrecht. For five summers, when I was aged between 11 and 15, I would spend up to a month in that country, playing with my many young cousins and their Dutch friends.

I'd heard of Ajax and Feyenoord of course, but I was curious to know who the local team were.

Someone told me it was PSV. They explained that they were only a small club, not very successful, and not very good.

The team had come a long way since then, and now they stood in the way of our Champions League progression.

They had been in the same group as us, earlier in the campaign. We had finished above them then, and hoped to do so again. And so it proved.

We managed to beat them both home and away, winning 3-0 at their ground and 1-0 at ours.

Our opponents in the next round, the semi-final itself, would be Chelsea again. Could history repeat itself?

Since Mourinho and Benitez took over at their respective clubs at the start of the 2004/2005 season, they had faced each other as managers on 15 separate occasions. They, and their teams, knew each other very well.

While Chelsea certainly had the ascendancy in the Premier League, we'd had our successes against them in the cup competitions.

At Stamford Bridge for the first leg, Chelsea had the better of the early exchanges and opened the scoring, through Joe Cole, on the half-hour mark.

Both keepers were called into action in the second half, but the match ended with the London club holding onto a 1-0 win.

The tie was delicately poised for the return game at Anfield.

Rafa Benitez, in his book 'Champions League dreams' said that he knew we would have the advantage of home support. The noise and the colour of 45,000 fans willing us on could startle Chelsea, as it had done two years before, when their players walked out into that cauldron of passion. He was hoping for the same effect again.

This time, though, Chelsea had a lead to defend, and if they could score just one goal, we would need to score three to go through to the final.

It would not be an easy night's work.

Benitez thought that our best way back into the tie might come from a set-piece. He had a few up his sleeve, and the ones he planned to use on the night were ones he'd not used in a while, knowing that Mourinho would be watching tapes of our recent matches in order to prepare.

Twenty minutes into the match, Liverpool won a free-kick just outside the Chelsea penalty area.

Most of our team rushed into the box. Steven Gerrard played a square ball to Daniel Agger, who was waiting just outside the area.

With the Chelsea defence occupied by our attackers in the box, Agger had the time and space to drill the ball low into the Chelsea goal.

The routine had worked. It was one that Benitez had only used once before, and that was in his Valencia days. Mourinho would have had to go back a number of years to have found it.

It was 1-0 to Liverpool on the night, and the same score to Rafa in his tactical duel with the Chelsea boss.

The tie, now all-square, went to extra-time.

The Reds had the better chances to score, hitting the cross-bar on one occasion.

The result would be decided on penalties.

We were at home. We had recently won both a Champions League final and the FA Cup from the 12-yard spot. We had nothing to fear.

Bolo Zenden went first for us. And scored.

Arjen Robben then had his shot saved by Pepe Reina, who had been well-drilled by the Liverpool coaches about where each of the Chelsea players might aim.

Xabi Alonso then fired home to make it 2-0 for us.

Lampard scored for them.

Gerrard scored for us.

Mourinho had brought on a penalty-taking expert, Geremi, late into extra-time.

Geremi shot. Pepe Reina saved.

If we scored with our next attempt, we would be going to Athens for the final.

Up stepped Dirk Kuyt.

The ball hit the back of the net.

The roof of the Kop nearly came off.

As the fans went wild in the stands, and the players went crazy on the pitch, Benitez walked calmly onto the pitch.

He was planning to pass on a few words of encouragement or tips to some of his squad. He was forever working, and forever thinking. I think the most you ever got out of him was a smile.

Craig Bellamy went running up to him, threw an arm around the gaffer's shoulder, and told him in no uncertain terms 'You are a f*cking genius!'

I wasn't at the game. I couldn't get a ticket, but I knew many people who were there.

After the match, I arranged to meet them in Hannah's Bar in town. I could walk there in five minutes from my flat.

And what a wonderful evening of celebration it was. We were off to another Champions League final, our second in three years. We sung our hearts out, hugging each other and jumping up and down.

'F*ck off, Chelsea FC. You aint got no history. Five European Cups, and 18 Leagues, that's what we call history!'

We had beaten Chelsea, and Mourinho, who had become enemy number one to the Liverpool fans.

This was no small feat considering Alex Ferguson was still on the scene.

Off to Athens we would go. Off to Athens I would go.

Our opponents would be AC Milan once more.

Once more unto the breach.

CHAPTER THIRTY-ONE

I didn't have a ticket for the Champions League final, but I decided to jump on a plane at the last minute leaving Liverpool for the Greek capital. I would get there about eight o'clock in the morning and would be leaving at about two in the morning the following day.

I had 18 hours to soak up the atmosphere and possibly find someone with a spare ticket. I would be meeting up with my dad and a few friends and family members. They all had tickets. I was chancing my arm, and following my old man's adage that all spare tickets ended up at the ground. That was the place to be if you wanted to get in.

As I made my way to the rendezvous with my dad and the others, I bumped into a couple of the five-a-side lads and spent a little time with them.

The streets were packed with Liverpool supporters. We far outnumbered the Italian fans, as far as I could tell.

The squares in the city were draped with our flags, and a crowd of people were enjoying the afternoon sun, merrily drinking, and singing football songs more usually heard on the Kop.

Here we were in Athens, painting the capital red.

After I'd met up with our lot, and the day wore on and edged towards the kick-off time, I moved closer and closer to the stadium, together with our group. I could feel the excitement building, but I also knew that I probably wouldn't get in.

'Any spares? Any spares?' I asked everyone who passed.

Then, as the security-ring tightened around the ground, I said my goodbyes and headed back into the city and found a pub where they were showing the match and where lots of other Liverpool fans had congregated.

The game kicked off. AC Milan – so gung-ho just two years earlier – were now much warier of the threat that we posed.

Their downfall in Istanbul had been to keep attacking when they were 3-0 up; such was their confidence in the superiority of their side that day.

There would be no repeat of that cavalier approach here.

In the first half of the match, The Reds were just about edging a tight game when the Italians were awarded a soft free-kick on the edge of our box, a minute before the interval.

Andrea Pirlo took it, and Pepe Reina in our goal looked to have it covered before the ball inadvertently struck Filippo Inzaghi, wrong-footed the keeper, and went in the back of the net.

It was just bad luck.

At the half-time break, Benitez urged the team to keep doing what they'd done for the first 45 minutes. We had been the better team.

In the second half, Liverpool had chances to level, but we could not grab that all-important equaliser.

With time running out, Rafa withdrew Javier Mascherano from midfield and sent on a striker, Peter Crouch.

Then Kaka, the AC Milan playmaker who had been expertly shackled by Mascherano for much of the game, now made the most of the freedom he'd been afforded by the Argentinian's withdrawal.

Finding himself in space, Kaka sent a pass into the path of Inzaghi to round Pepe Reina and fire into an empty net for his and Milan's second goal of the night.

With just one minute of normal play remaining, Dirk Kuyt scored with a header.

Could we do what we had done in Istanbul and peg them back again?

There were three minutes of injury time announced on the board.

Carlo Ancelotti, the Milan manager, made a substitution, which should have added another 30 seconds to the time to be played.

After just two minutes and 45 seconds of time added on, and with Liverpool on the attack and looking for that second and equalising goal, the German referee blew up for the final whistle.

Milan had taken their revenge for their night of misery at the Ataturk. Now, the misery was all ours.

Benitez approached the referee, Herbert Fandel.

'You blew early,' he told him, but the referee didn't want to know.

It was game over.

Season over.

There would be no third cup in three years for Rafa.

Benitez returned to the team hotel. Together with his chief scout, he analysed what had gone wrong and what they planned to put right going forward.

They went over every decision in the game they had just lost, both tactically and technically, as they tried to think about what they might have done differently.

The next morning, Rafa had to face the world's press. He was not in a good mood. How could he be after the disappointment of the previous night's match?

He wasted no time in telling the assembled journalists that if the club were serious about winning the Premier League, they would have to spend money. Serious money.

He had identified the targets that he wanted to bring in, and now it was time for the owners to act.

Top of his list was the Atletico Madrid forward Fernando Torres. He was the player to take us to the next level and allow us to compete in the league with Man Utd and Chelsea.

It was no use battling to make third or fourth place each year. We needed to win the Premier League to show we were back to our best.

Torres would cost £20 million and would prove to be worth every penny. He was our most expensive signing ever, and this would serve as a statement of intent.

Also incoming were Ryan Babel and Yossi Benayoun to give us more options up front.

Out would go Craig Bellamy, off to play his golf elsewhere.

The 2007/2008 season began and saw Liverpool as the early pacemakers.

Torres arrived like a force of nature, his speed and precision catching other Premier League teams unawares.

We remained unbeaten until December when successive defeats to Reading and Man Utd served as a reality check.

Still, we were up near the top of the table and remained in contention. We appeared to be making progress.

Off the pitch, however, things weren't going nearly so well.

As was the case before, when we had tried to work with two managers in Evans and Houllier, we were now coming unstuck with joint-chairmen in Gillett and Hicks.

Benitez had tried to build on our blistering start by identifying further improvements that we could make in the coming January transfer window.

He reiterated his earlier message to the owners that we had to move quickly to secure his targets, before other clubs got wind of them and maybe stepped in to steal the players we wanted from under our noses.

Rafa received a terse email in reply from Tom Hicks, in capital letters no less, telling him to concentrate on the coaching and to work with the players he had.

Relations at the top became frosty, to say the least.

We finished the calendar year in third place and, in the transfer window, brought in Martin Skrtel in defence and also turned Mascherano's loan-deal into a permanent signing.

Still, relations between the manager and the owners were strained.

Benitez also heard on the grapevine that Hicks and Gillett had sounded out Jurgen Klinsmann about taking Rafa's job.

When quizzed if this was true, the owners told Benitez that they had merely met him to discuss some marketing ideas.

Yes. Right!

Maybe they were going to give him a stall outside the ground and get him to sell some scarves.

'Hats, scarves, or a badge,' all shouted with a German accent.

Back in the league, January brought three draws and a defeat, away to West Ham.

We then won six of our next seven matches before we were again brought crashing back to earth at Old Trafford, losing 3-0 after a harsh sending off for Mascherano made an already difficult task nigh-on impossible.

We closed out the season with five wins and two draws, but could only finish in fourth place.

We'd gone out of the League Cup in December, and the FA Cup in February.

That still left the Champions League.

We had progressed from a tough group, and defeated Inter Milan and then Arsenal in the knockout stages.

We had reached another semi-final where our opponents would be, yes, Chelsea again!

We had beaten them at the same point in the competition in two of the previous three years.

We appeared to have them jinxed; however, our winning streak was about to come to an end.

It looked like we would win the first-leg at Anfield courtesy of a Dirk Kuyt goal; however, John Arne Riise hooked the ball into his own net deep into injury time.

It was a cruel blow. Chelsea now had an away goal to take back to Stamford Bridge, and our job had just got a whole lot harder.

In the return leg, Didier Drogba scored first for The Blues, before Fernando Torres equalised to take the game to extra-time.

Lampard then scored from the penalty spot, and Drogba added another.

Liverpool kept fighting, and Ryan Babel scored with a speculative long-range effort late-on, but Chelsea held on for the win.

They were headed to the final of the Champions League. If they were to win, they would become the first London club to ever do so.

Their opponents for the final, to be played in Moscow, would be none other than Manchester United.

We couldn't help but think about what might have been. We could have faced our greatest rivals for the greatest prize in club football. It would have been the game of the century.

If we had won that game, we could have lorded it over United forever. If we had lost, they would never have let us live it down. Nothing else would have mattered.

I don't think we bottled it. I think our luck just ran out against Chelsea.

We had been their hoodoo club in the competition in previous seasons, but now they had got their revenge.

That season, our Reserves-side had won their version of the Premier League.

The first team longed to do the same.

We had waited almost two decades to be crowned champions of England, and we were *still* behind Arsenal, Chelsea, and Man Utd. There was plenty of ground to make up.

The club had made a profit of almost £30 million on player transfers in the previous season, and we were becoming a selling rather than a buying club at a time when we needed to improve.

Benitez was at odds with the owners. That much was clear to see.

The fans gave their backing to the manager, and made their feelings about Hicks and Gillett known.

Fernando Torres had done well, scoring 33 times in all competitions, but we had no cups and just a fourth-place league finish to show for it.

Benitez was now entering his fifth year as Liverpool manager. Recent history had shown that this would be definitive.

Despite a good start to his time as Reds boss, and the support that he got from the fans, the pressure was mounting on Rafa to deliver the prize the fans most wanted.

We *had* to win the Premier League.

CHAPTER THIRTY-TWO

When Liverpool last won the league title, back in 1990, it was the 18th time that we had won the competition, which was far and away a record. We stood head and shoulders above everybody else.

At that time, Chelsea had only ever won it once since the club was founded in 1905. When Jose Mourinho led the team to the title in 2005, it had been 50 years exactly since their only previous victory.

Similarly, back in 1990, Man Utd had notched up just seven title wins in their entire history.

Come the start of the 2008/2009 season, though, United were now right behind us with 17 title wins. Win it again and they would equal our record.

How had we let them catch us up when we had been so far out in front? In the time that we had been stagnant, they had been sprinting.

We now needed a blistering start in the league to give us any hope of keeping our noses out in front.

As the season began, we initially managed to do just that.

We won seven and drew three of our opening ten games, which included victories over both of our main competitors in Chelsea and Man Utd.

A reverse to Tottenham in early November was the only blot on an otherwise perfect copy-book.

After that small hiccup, we quickly picked up the pace again, winning five and drawing four of our next nine games to end the calendar year at the top of the league.

Then came Rafa's infamous 'rant' when, out of the blue, he decided to launch an attack on Alex Ferguson at a press conference, outlining several 'facts' about how Fergie exerted undue influence on referees and played psychological tricks on opposition managers.

If this was Benitez's attempt to engage Fergie in mind games, then it sadly failed, as it seemed to have a galvanising effect on United. It turned the spotlight back onto a Liverpool side who, but for the ensuing furore, might have stolen a lead as we entered the all-important second half of the season.

Having set ourselves up for a fall, we then drew our next three matches, leaving the door to the title race ajar and allowing Man Utd to claim the top spot.

Despite losing only once throughout the remainder of the campaign, we still trailed in a disappointing second.

We had blown the best chance we'd had in years of winning the league.

We had beaten our fiercest rivals both home and away, including a memorable 4-1 trouncing of the Red Devils at Old Trafford, where Steven Gerrard ran up to a TV camera in the aftermath of one of the goals, and famously planted a kiss onto the screen.

It would be bettered a few months later when Man Utd fans posted their own images of Ryan Giggs lifting and kissing the Premier League trophy. Which one would you prefer?

In the Champions League, we had shown we were a match for anyone on our day as we beat the mighty Real Madrid 1-0 at the Bernabeu before demolishing them again in the return leg by four goals to nil at Anfield.

It was a highlight, a glorious memory, but it wasn't a trophy.

We finished the Premier League season with 86 points, our highest-ever tally. We still ended up in second place.

After beating Real Madrid, we then went out of the Champions League at the quarter-final stage when we faced our perennial opponents, Chelsea.

Were we making progress and getting closer, or would the prize we craved most of all remain out of reach?

United's league title meant we were now both equal on 18 wins. If we didn't achieve the top spot in the 2009/2010 season, it would represent two full decades of failure in the competition that we had once called our own.

Even worse, if United won it again, they'd have broken our record.

Benitez believed that the second-placed finish showed how good we could be. Some small changes were needed to improve the team and the squad, but we had been consistent, losing only twice all season, and our points tally and the number of goals we had scored were proof that we were almost there.

Behind the scenes though, Benitez said he felt more like a bank manager than a football manager.

Hicks and Gillett had hugely leveraged the club with loans, specifically from the Royal Bank of Scotland (RBS), in order to raise the initial funds to purchase the football club. These were short-term loans taken out with high interest rates and, with the world in financial meltdown at the time, RBS wanted and needed their money back. And the owners of Liverpool didn't have it.

Benitez wanted funds to buy certain players but, if the owners couldn't pay the bank the money that they owed them, they certainly couldn't be seen to be funding improvements to the team.

We had, sadly, reached our peak under Benitez.

We had also reached the end of our tether with Hicks and Gillett.

The fans wanted them gone. The manager and the players wanted them gone.

The banks began to call in the loans and started to search for new owners, someone who could pay off the debt that was owed to them

Supporters hoped that, whoever these new owners were, they would have enough money behind them to both clear our debts and still support the team on the pitch.

Benitez realised that no-one was coming to his aid. He could not get answers from the chairmen or directors. The transatlantic lines of communication had gone dead.

He tried to put these issues to one side and focussed all of his energy on the players, to extract every ounce of effort from the squad in order to make the jump from second to first place in the league.

It was not to be. There was just too much negativity around the club. The owners were at odds with the banks. The fans were at odds with the owners. The players didn't really know what was going on behind the scenes, but the lack of any recent signings told its own story.

Critics were now labelling us a two-man team, in Steven Gerrard and Fernando Torres. This was a little harsh. Pepe Reina was pretty good too!

Out on the pitch, as the season got underway, nothing seemed to go our way.

We lost two of our opening three league games.

We won our next four games, but this was hardly unexpected for a team that had finished as runners-up in the previous campaign.

We then lost to Chelsea and, in the next match, we lost 1-0 to Sunderland via a goal that went in off a beach ball!

A young Liverpool fan, trying to inject some humour into our dour season, threw the offending item onto the pitch where it landed in our penalty area.

Darren Bent, for The Black Cats, had a shot at goal. Pepe Reina stooped to collect it, before the ball took a huge deflection off the inflatable, and ended up in the back of the net.

And the referee saw nothing wrong with it, even though it was against the rules of the game.

If there is clear outside interference, the game should have been stopped.

I know I sound like Victor Meldrew here but, a beach ball diverting the ball into the net? If that's not outside interference, I don't know what is.

Our bad luck was reaching ridiculous proportions. I simply couldn't believe it!

We won just half of our first 20 fixtures to finish the calendar year in seventh place. We were also out of the Champions League by early December, failing to make it out of the group stage for the first time in seven years.

The second half of the season was similarly disappointing, despite a run to the semi-finals of the Europa League.

In the Premiership, we won fewer than half of our remaining fixtures and trailed in a (still) lowly seventh. To make matters worse, the title-winners were Man Utd.

They had now surpassed our number of wins and stood alone at the summit with a magnificent 19 titles.

We had lost our crown.

What we hadn't lost was our manager. Rafa Benitez had signed a new five-year contract at the end of the previous season. It was neither his nor the owners' idea. The request had come directly from the Royal Bank of Scotland in order to provide some stability at a time when the club was clearly going through a difficult period.

Off the field, Hicks and Gillett had finally agreed to sell the club. They simply could not hold those toxic loans at bay any longer.

Martin Broughton took over from the Texas cowboys as club chairman. He called Benitez into his office to hear the manager's plans for the future. Rafa explained that he wanted the chance to rebuild the squad, get Liverpool back into the Champions League places, and try to win the Premier League for all of The Reds' supporters.

It was not to be. Broughton had already made his mind up, for reasons best known to himself. Rafa's departure was described as the obligatory 'by mutual consent'. It wasn't. It was a club decision that Rafa had little choice but to accept.

The club statement thanked the manager for all of his hard work and said he would always be a part of Anfield folklore after that incredible Champions League win in Istanbul. 'But,' it went on to say, 'after a disappointing season, both parties felt a fresh start would be best for all concerned.'

That was certainly not how Benitez saw it. He just wanted the club to sort out its ownership and money troubles and then back him so we could compete for the big prizes.

He would not have the chance.

Though he had produced the miracle of Istanbul that night on the Bosphorus, Rafa was no longer the boss for us.

It was time for new owners, and a new manager.

It had been 20 years since we had last won the title.

All the fans wanted, and all the fans hoped, was that the new owners and the new manager would match our ambition.

We wanted to win the Premier League.

CHAPTER THIRTY-THREE

On the 1st of July 2010, it was announced that the new Liverpool manager would be (drumroll, please) Roy Hodgson. We had replaced Rafa Benitez, who had won La Liga in Spain (twice), a UEFA Cup, a Champions League, and the FA Cup, with a man whose last major honour was a Danish league title ten years earlier.

It didn't make much sense. Fans were left a little gobsmacked and decidedly underwhelmed.

In fact, for his first game in charge in front of the Kop, there wasn't even the usual rousing reception. Nobody sang his name. There was nothing. Maybe it was a case of 'Let's see how you do.'

The omens weren't good to begin with. The first match of the club's pre-season tour was cancelled when the heavens opened in biblical proportions beforehand, and flooded the pitch.

The season itself got off to a similarly poor start with four defeats in our first eight matches to leave us in the relegation zone.

We had been beaten at home by Blackpool. If that wasn't bad enough, we then lost 2-0 to Everton, our bitter rivals from across Stanley Park.

Hodgson said he thought we'd played some great football, if only in the second half of that stinging defeat.

The press conference in which Hodgson shared those views took place in a room at Goodison straight after the game. They had to close the windows to drown out the noise of the Everton fans outside, who were gleefully singing 'Going down, going down, going down!'

When Alex Ferguson then said that he thought Hodgson was doing a good job at Liverpool, you knew how awful things had become. If Man Utd had a manager who was leading them to relegation, every Reds supporter in the land would want him knighted.

For his first League Cup game in charge of The Reds, against fourth division Northampton Town, Hodgson declared that we faced a 'formidable challenge'. If that was the case, then great European nights were going to be a thing of the past.

In fact, Roy's words proved to be prophetic, as Northampton knocked us out of the cup, and at Anfield no less!

Liverpool then won three league games in succession to move up to ninth in the table. It was a respite of sorts, but it turned out to be brief.

After consecutive defeats at Newcastle and then at home to bottom of the table Wolverhampton Wanderers, Hodgson suggested that our supporters should get used to such results. We were to lower our expectations, rather than him raising his.

In all, we would win just three of our next nine games, and these were to be Hodgson's last matches in charge. He was sacked in early January after an away defeat at Blackburn.

His tenure had lasted a total of six months, and that includes the pre-season. It was by far the shortest managerial reign in the club's history.

When he'd joined us in the summer, he had rented his property from an estate agent, who happened to be a friend of mine. She had asked him, when showing him around, what he liked to do in his spare time.

Hodgson said that he and his wife (who was, incidentally, a Scouser, though an Evertonian), liked to go to the theatre, especially the smaller, quirkier ones.

My friend Sue told him that her friend (i.e. me) had put on a production at one of the city's fringe theatres just a few weeks earlier. In fact, I had rented a couple of her apartments to accommodate some of my actors.

I was quite thrilled to think that the manager of Liverpool was getting to hear about my work.

I liked Roy Hodgson. I thought he was a lovely man. I just didn't want him running (and ruining) my football team.

You can make all of the excuses that you like for Hodgson's time in charge. It wasn't his team; he didn't have enough time; he never had the backing of the fans, etc.

The truth is that neither the players nor the supporters ever responded to him. We were languishing near the bottom of the table, and he didn't seem to understand how embarrassing this was to a club of our stature. There was no sense of *urgency* from the manager. He seemed to think this was the norm, when it absolutely wasn't.

Off-the-field pressures simply added to the malaise. At one point, the situation between the owners and the bank could have seen the club placed into administration. According to the rules of the Football League, this would have brought with it an automatic nine-point deduction.

Given our perilous position in the table, it would almost certainly have seen the club relegated from the Premiership. It just didn't bear thinking about.

The fans only started to sing Roy's name in December, and then it was only to make their feelings clear.

'Hodgson for England,' they shouted, with no shortage of irony.

There was also another name on their lips.

That of King Kenny.

Even in the 1990s, Kenny had apparently let it be known, through his connections with the club, that he would be willing to come back as manager.

Or, rather, that he was desperate to come back.

He was now working at Anfield again in an ambassadorial role. When Rafa Benitez was removed from the post, Dalglish came out and told the Chairman and Chief Executive that he was actively interested in the job.

Rightly or wrongly, the directors said that they wanted Kenny to take a more senior and long-term position with the club. If they appointed him manager, and then it didn't work out, they would lose him altogether.

Yet, when Hodgson's time with the club came to an end, it was Dalglish that they turned to.

The Kop had been heard.

At the time, I was working in Warrington. There were six of us in the office. The manager was an Evertonian. Then there was me. The other four were all Man Utd fans.

Asked by a colleague what I thought of Kenny's appointment, I said only this.

'I'm not going to sit here and say that we're going to win this, that, and the other, this year, that year, or the next. All I can tell you is that I'm really, really *happy*.'

And I was. And I did think that we would win all of those things, but I didn't want to put a time or date on any of it. I was just happy. And that went for a lot of us.

In his very first press conference back in charge, the first question that Kenny got asked was, 'Are you in a relegation battle?'

Sitting just four points above the drop-zone, we most certainly were, but Dalglish wasn't going to say that. He said 'no'.

He wanted his team looking up, not down.

He lost and drew his first two league games, and then won the next four on the bounce.

We lost only two of our next ten matches, winning six times in that period.

We were now safely in the top half of the table. Kenny was right. What relegation battle?

The King had also had a busy introduction to the transfer market. Fernando Torres had decided that he wanted to leave in January.

Torres had not had a good first half to the season. To be honest, his form had dipped in the season before as well. It had all the hallmarks of a player who no longer wanted to be at the club. In fact, he had produced only one decent performance in the current campaign when he scored two great first-half goals as we beat Chelsea at Anfield.

And who did Torres want to move to? Yes, Chelsea. He was clearly putting himself in the shop window. It was proof that he could still do it when he wanted to; he just no longer wanted to do it for us.

I'd gone to that game, and I had stood in the away end. This wasn't something I would normally do, and it's definitely not something I'd recommend!

My mate from university was a Chelsea fan and he was coming up for the game. Did I want to meet him near the train station in town for a pint before the match?

Of course, I said.

While we were having a drink, he mentioned that he had a spare ticket. Did I want it?

Why not? It would be in the Chelsea end, but I'd be with my good mate, and I wouldn't say or do anything stupid. It would be fine. I was entitled to watch my own team in my own city. Or so I thought.

We went to the game. We presented our tickets and entered the away section of the ground in the Anfield Road end.

We were walking up the steps, looking for our seats when my mate, Michael, said 'Right, you're over there!'

The bugger hadn't told me that the seats weren't together.

It turned out that we were on the same row, but about 20 seats apart.

I found myself next to the cheerleaders of the 'Zigger-Zagger, Zigger-Zagger, Oi, Oi, Oi' chant.

Then Torres scored twice, two crackers, and both right in front of me.

I didn't say a word. I even tried to look as disconsolate as all of the Chelsea fans around me.

Then, about 15 minutes into the second half, noticing my lack of involvement in the chanting and the ritual abuse of the Liverpool players and their fans, one of the gentlemen (I'm using the term loosely) beside me, turned and asked 'Why are you 'ere?'

What could I say?

There were three young lads on the other side of me. They'd been speaking a foreign language for the last hour. Should I pretend to be French like them?

I thought about responding to the question with 'Je ne vous comprends pas,' perhaps before turning to the lads next to me and saying 'Quelle heure est-il maintenant?' to give the impression that I was part of their group.

I wasn't quite sure if there was a hint of Scouse to my French accent though, so I gave that idea a miss.

I considered responding instead with 'I'm just wotchin the game, mate' in my best (or possibly worst) Cockney accent.

That was probably worse than trying to speak French.

So, I simply said, 'I'm just watching the game.'

He looked shocked, as if I'd just announced 'I am an alien.'

'But you're a Scouser,' he said, incredulous.

'Yes,' I explained, 'but I'm here with my Chelsea mate.'

'Yes,' he said, 'but you are a Scouser.'

'Yes,' I repeated, 'but I'm here with my Chelsea mate.'

'Yes,' he said (and we could probably have done this all week) 'but you're not Chelsea. You're a Scouser.'

He then turned to his mate and announced that there was a Scouser amongst them. In fact, within touching (and punching) distance.

His mate goes 'Noooo?' He was similarly incredulous.

Well, the news took all of about five seconds to ripple through about 3,000 Chelsea fans, all of whom were now staring in my direction; wishing, threatening, and attempting to get within strangling distance of me.

Hmmm. It was time to think. This wasn't looking good.

The lad in front of me then turned around and asked 'Are you a Scouser?'

'Yes,' I replied.

He looked like he was about to say something nasty, then he recognised a fellow human being and instead said 'Oh, boy, you are in so much trouble.'

He was looking behind me, where I could only imagine that people were scrambling over seats to get at me.

The lad next to me, the one who first rumbled me, then grabbed me in a headlock.

I shrugged him off me.

Impertinent man!

I then decided I'd better go and find Michael.

I pushed past the Zigger-Zagger boys and made my way towards the bank of steps that separated us and then along the row until I squeezed in beside my mate.

'It's on top over there,' I said, by way of explanation.

Hate-filled eyes had followed me to my new seat.

The supporters were all standing up as they watched the game, with no-one actually using the expensive seats, so I was able to get in next to Mick.

'You shouldn't be in here,' said the bloke behind me.

'But I haven't said anything,' I explained. I'd kept my mouth shut the whole time, not celebrated our goals or anything of the sort.

'It don't matter. You shouldn't be in here,' the bloke behind me repeated.

A match steward then approached me.

'You've got to leave,' he said.

'But I haven't said anything,' I said again.

'I know, but there's a load of stewards and police holding back a mob of about 50 lads who want to kill you. You've got to go for everyone's safety.'

Well, there wasn't much that I could say to that.

Me and Michael headed for the steps that would take us down towards the pitch and the exit. That meant heading back towards the waiting mob.

As we started to descend, one young lad, whose inanities I'd endured for the whole of the match as he called my team, my city, and my compatriots everything under the sun, then tried to intimidate me, waving his arms in a ridiculous gesture.

I laughed in his face and hoped his mates would give him stick all the way home. As if I wasn't terrified enough, my life in mortal danger, and he has to try and intimidate me.

Then, a giant of a man came bounding down the steps behind me, his arm arcing behind him about to clobber me right over the head.

The blow would probably have killed me.

Luckily, Michael is six foot three and was stood between us.

He stopped the man in his tracks by simply saying 'F*ck off. He's with me.'

'Oh,' the bloke said, and he immediately pulled his arm back and halted the attempted assault.

Michael and I left the ground and went to the Arkles pub opposite and watched the last 20 minutes of the match in there.

So those goals were the highlight of Fernando Torres' last season with us, and were almost the end of my Anfield career too!

Reluctantly, Dalglish took the money for Torres and used some of it to buy Andy Carroll. The rest he put towards signing the Ajax forward Luis Suarez.

We got £50 million for Fernando Torres, which was shrewd business for a player who had cost us £20 million. We also got two new strikers for the money.

It had always been Dalglish's philosophy that the money was no good to him sitting in the bank. He wanted to see it out on the pitch.

So did the fans.

Luckily for us, there would be plenty to see going forward.

Dalglish had averted the potential disaster of relegation and had steadied the ship in his first few months back in charge.

What could he do with a whole season ahead of him?

I, for one, couldn't wait to find out.

CHAPTER THIRTY-FOUR

The appointment of Kenny Dalglish came against the backdrop of upheaval concerning the ownership of the club.

Hicks and Gillett had been due to repay their loans to RBS in April of 2010. They were unable to do so and, instead, took out a six-month extension to their financing which would last until October of that year. This time, it came with an additional £60 million penalty if they were unable to make the payment.

To ensure financial fair-play, the bank had insisted that a five-member board be instituted to oversee either the raising of further funds or the sale of the club to new owners.

Together with Hicks and Gillet, the board consisted of Ian Ayre, the club's commercial director, Christian Purslow, the club's managing director, and Martin Broughton, the club chairman. Broughton also held the casting vote in the event of a split vote on the issue of sale.

New England Sports Ventures (NESV), owners of the Boston Red Sox, and led by John Henry and Tom Werner, were the only prospective buyers.

When it became apparent that they would not stump up the sums that Hicks and Gillett wanted, and that Ayre, Purslow, and Broughton were inclined to accept the offer, Hicks and Gillett simply kicked the three men off the board and replaced them with two members of their own company.

RBS took the case to the Royal Court of Justice where it was agreed that, subject to the conditions of the six-month loan extension, Hicks and Gillett had given up the right to remove members of the board arbitrarily.

The three ousted members would be re-instated. The sale to NESV would go through.

In a further desperate throw of the dice, Hicks and Gillett took out an injunction in a court in Texas to prevent the sale of a valuable asset at a price they were not happy with.

The injunction was initially granted, but it didn't go down well with the Texas judge when he found out that the case had already been decided, in a Royal Court no less.

In the UK, Lord Justice Floyd despatched Hicks and Gillett back to Texas to have the injunction withdrawn.

The sale to NESV could now go through, but not before Tom Hicks issued a statement that he would sue Liverpool Football Club for $1 billion for the illegal sale.

It was just more bluster. It had been bluster all along, and Hicks later dropped the case.

Out went the owners. In came the new.

Americans again, but cut from a different cloth.

The owners changed their corporate name from NESV to the Fenway Sports Group (FSG), after Fenway Park, home of the Boston Red Sox baseball team, which they also owned.

After they purchased the baseball club in 2002, within two seasons, the club won their first World Championship in 86 years.

It was a good omen for the red team on Merseyside, who were also looking to get back to winning ways.

Our new owners, John W Henry and Tom Werner, were not just pin-striped and cold-blooded businessmen. As a young man, John Henry had failed to graduate from college as he was playing in a rock and roll band and had put his undoubted energies and focus into that. He later started trading on the American stock exchange, and made his money there.

Tom Werner was a television producer whose expertise was in comedy. He had been responsible for the development of groundbreaking hits such as Mork and Mindy, Soap, Taxi, Roseanne, and Third Rock from the Sun.

I remember an early radio interview that Werner conducted, not long after FSG took over LFC.

When asked what the plan for the club was, Werner replied that he wanted the club's wage bill to go up.

'Up?' asked the surprised broadcaster.

'Yes,' Werner replied.

He explained that there was a clear correlation between wages and success. Better wages attracted better players. Better players equalled more chance of success on the pitch.

The interviewer didn't quite believe him.

'So,' he said, 'you wouldn't mind buying a player for such-and-such amount of money.' (He mentioned a figure of about £50 million.)

Werner responded by saying that he had personally signed a cheque for an American baseball player for $100 million. He added 'I might not have liked doing it, but I knew that I had to, in order to help create a winning team.'

On hearing that, I knew that we were in good hands. This was a management team with ambition, not fazed by the size of the task ahead of them, and determined to deliver success.

The radio interview had been about business, and about football, and Werner had responded in depth to the well-prepared barrage of questions.

'Gee,' he said, as the interview came to an end, 'and I never even got to show you that I have a sense of humour too.'

He'd been constrained by the questions. He had so much more to give.

These new owners had clout and personality. They also had the money that we needed to move on from our recent misery and make headway towards the good times.

Their interest in Liverpool came when one of their trusted lieutenants sent John Henry an email titled 'Save my club'.

Life-long Liverpool fan Joe Januszewski was an executive at the Red Sox, where he was known affectionately as 'The Soccer Guy' as he was forever talking about LFC.

Henry and Werner heard that English football offered a great investment opportunity. They asked Joe to elaborate on this for them, in the form of an email. And he did.

Their interest in the club could not have come at a more opportune moment, for them and for Liverpool.

It took just 60 days from receipt of that email for FSG to complete the takeover at Anfield.

There was no doubting their ability to deliver in the boardroom. Now, we just needed them to match our ambition on the pitch.

Within two months of taking over the club, the new owners dispatched with the services of team manager, Roy Hodgson.

Henry and Werner were artistic and creative people at heart. No doubt they felt the vibe coming from the fans and decided to act fast. Plus, they didn't want to buy the club and see it slip immediately out of the Premiership. After all, you can't win a competition that you aren't even in!

Out went Roy Hodgson. In came a man just four years his junior in Kenny Dalglish.

Maybe the new owners were buying themselves a little time as they took stock of their new acquisition.

Dalglish, though, was here to win.

Everyone who had ever watched him play, saw how he managed his teams, or who heard his inspirational oratory would expect nothing less from him.

As Kenny himself once said, 'Show me a good loser and I'll show you a loser.'

Winning was everything.

Winning for Liverpool football club meant everything and more.

With the new (and right) owners now in place, and the new (and right) manager in charge, what could we go on to achieve?

First, it was stability. We had finished sixth in the league. Respectable, given where we were when Dalglish took over. There would be no more talk of relegation.

But what would come next?

Did we dare to dream again?

It was time to find out.

CHAPTER THIRTY-FIVE

Back in the hot seat, one of the first things that Dalglish did was to appoint fellow-Scot Steve Clarke as assistant manager.

Clarke came with a great pedigree. He had previously held the same position under Jose Mourinho at Chelsea, and in his three seasons in the role saw the club lift two Premier League titles, two League Cups, and the FA Cup.

He then moved to West Ham to work alongside Gianfranco Zola. Chelsea refused his resignation and then sought compensation worth two years of Clarke's salary. He was clearly highly thought of at the West London club.

Clarke left The Hammers in June 2010 and was appointed as Dalglish's assistant just two days after Kenny took the reins.

Together, the two Scotsmen aimed to take Liverpool to the top of the pile.

Dalglish had always sought out the best up-and-coming players. In a previous incarnation, during his first stint as a manager, he had often gone head-to-head with Alex Ferguson as they vied to buy the best players they could find.

Kenny and Fergie had fought for the signatures of Roy Keane and Alan Shearer. They ended up with one apiece.

Now, the scouts were pointing at a young man from Sunderland called Jordan Henderson.

For £16 million, he signed on the dotted line for Liverpool. Fergie claimed he didn't want him anyway. The lad had a poor running gait which might pose him problems down the line. He bought Phil Jones from Blackburn instead.

We also brought in Charlie Adam in midfield and, on the left-wing, Stewart Downing from Aston Villa for £20 million.

Up front, Craig Bellamy returned to the club on a free transfer from Man City. Bellamy was a lifelong Liverpool fan. To come back to the club, and to play under his idol Dalglish, was wish-fulfilment of the higher-order.

It was now time to do the same for the fans.

The season kicked off with a draw and two wins for The Reds. We then slumped to two defeats away from home. The first was against Stoke, where Jonathan Walters scored the only goal of the game. It would be the first of seven career-strikes that he would get against Liverpool, for whom he became a bit of a bogey-man.

Our next loss was at Tottenham where we found ourselves reduced to nine men after two sendings-off and the result was a resounding, though unsurprising in the circumstances, 4-0 defeat.

We then won our next two matches to go up to fifth-place in the league.

The next game would be a 1-1 draw against Man Utd at Anfield. Luis Suarez was accused of racially abusing Patrice Evra on the pitch, a charge which he denied, but one which he would have to defend at a Football Association hearing that was scheduled for December.

Two wins and three draws before our next defeat, away to Fulham, meant we had gone nearly three months without losing in the league.

Liverpool then won their next two matches, before the findings of Suarez's racism hearing were announced.

The result was a guilty verdict. Suarez was fined £40,000 and banned for eight matches.

The club considered an appeal. They denounced racism of any kind, but said they still believed Suarez to have been innocent, as he had vehemently protested.

Suarez was still free to play in the fortnight the club were granted to consider their appeal.

We drew twice and won once to end 2011 in sixth place.

On the 3rd of January, Liverpool FC said that they would accept the FA's punishment of the Uruguayan. They still did not believe in his guilt, but they did not want to drag the case out, or appear to take an issue as important as racism lightly.

The transcripts of the hearing stated that, during the game, there was a coming together in the penalty box between the players as a corner was being taken.

There was some pushing and shoving, and Evra said to Suarez, 'Don't touch me, you South American,' to which Suarez replied, 'Why, because you are black?'

Suarez had then shrugged his shoulders to indicate this had been a question, and not intended as an insult.

The FA felt otherwise. Suarez was banned.

The result put a dampener on the whole mood at the club, as well it might. It also seemed to affect our league form, as we won just five, drew four, and lost 11 of our remaining 19 matches from the start of the year until the end of the season.

We finished in eighth place overall, but that wasn't the real story of Kenny's first campaign back in charge.

In order to create a team of winners, Dalglish had targeted silverware, and here he'd had much more success.

In the League Cup, we had overcome Exeter, Brighton and Hove Albion, and Stoke City in the early rounds.

We'd then faced Chelsea at Stamford Bridge and beat them by two goals to nil to set up a two-legged semi-final against Manchester City.

A 1-0 away win in the first tie meant we were just one game away from an appearance at Wembley.

A 2-2 draw in the return fixture put us in the League Cup final, where we would face Cardiff City.

On the 26th of February, we stepped out onto the pitch at the new Wembley stadium. Due to previous finals being relocated to the Millennium Stadium, it would be our first appearance at the London venue for 16 years!

The match ended 1-1 after 90 minutes, and 2-2 after extra-time.

Liverpool missed the first two of their penalties. Cardiff had scored one of theirs.

Then Kuyt scored, Stewart Downing scored, and Glen Johnson scored for The Reds, while Cardiff missed two more of theirs; the last of them by Steven Gerrard's cousin, Anthony, playing for The Bluebirds.

It was our first trophy for six years. We would soon have the chance of another as we had also reached the final of the FA Cup.

Along the way, we had beaten Oldham, old-rivals Man Utd, Brighton, Stoke, and – in a semi-final played at Wembley – Everton,

In order to cover the cost of building the new stadium, the FA decided that all semi-finals, as well as the final of the cup, should be played at their new home.

In the semi, Everton took the lead, but Liverpool never gave up.

Sylvain Distin, in The Toffees' defence, chased a ball towards the touch-line. Suarez made to go with him but, with the defender looking the other way, peeled off and raced towards the Everton goal.

Distin attempted a back-pass, Suarez intercepted it and raced towards Tim Howard in the Everton goal. Before he even reached the box, the Uruguayan hit the ball with the outside of his right boot, and it swerved unerringly into the bottom corner of the net, past Howard's outstretched hand. We were back in the game.

Then, with just three minutes left on the clock and the cup final heading for extra-time, Andy Carroll flicked a backwards header into the Everton goal.

We won the game 2-1.

In the final itself, we were up against Chelsea, at the time one of the top two teams in England. There was a lot of recent history between us, and not a lot of love.

Chelsea took an early lead through Ramires and went into the interval 1-0 up.

In the second half, Frank Lampard rounded young Liverpool midfielder Jay Spearing and set up Drogba to score Chelsea's second of the match.

It was clear that the experienced Lampard had the beating of our young central midfielder. Dalglish made an immediate change and replaced Spearing with Andy Carroll, who had been left on the bench.

Carroll scored within ten minutes of coming on which begged the question – probably more for the owners than anyone else – why did our £35 million striker not start the match?

After 81 minutes of play, Carroll thought that he had scored again. His header appeared to have crossed the line, and he peeled away in celebration, but referee Phil Dowd, having consulted with his linesman, decided not to award it.

Without the benefit of goal-line technology, I guess we'll never know. What I do know is that the match ultimately ended in a 2-1 Chelsea victory and, soon, that it would rob Dalglish of another season or more in charge of the club.

Had he won that cup final, which would have been his second trophy of the season, it would surely have been impossible for the owners to part company with him. And why would they want to?

However, the decision to go with an inexperienced midfielder, and leave a star-striker on the bench, in a match that we ultimately lost, meant that they had ample opportunity to focus on the negatives of what was still Kenny's first full season back in charge.

Our league form was steady. We were doing okay. The worst results came about while Suarez was banned and when Liverpool were winning in the cup competitions.

I'm convinced that Dalglish was just blooding his players, showing them how to get across the finish line and pick up a medal and a trophy. Once they had acquired that knack, he could ask them to continue in this way throughout an entire league campaign.

You have to start somewhere.

Take a player like Stewart Downing. He was a talented winger, but he failed to show up for many of the league games. I couldn't bear to watch him. He didn't have the fight in his belly, week in and week out. I would curse him. Literally curse him from the stands. He was so frustrating to watch.

Then, in the cup games, those quarters and semi-finals of the League Cup and FA Cup, he played like a man possessed. Dalglish had lit a fire under him. For those 90 minutes, he was unstoppable. I was awestruck.

Downing won himself a League Cup medal and helped us reach the final of the FA Cup where we ran Chelsea incredibly close. On another day, Andy Carroll's second attempt on goal might have been given. We might have won a cup-double.

Imagine what those players, now versed in the art of winning, might have done in the next campaign.

I'm sure the league would have been the main focus for Dalglish and Steve Clarke in the coming season.

Instead, Kenny was called to the offices of John W Henry in Boston and told that the club wished to relieve him of his duties.

Of all the things I wish I had done in my life, this is my Liverpool one.

I wish I'd have gone to Boston and sat in Henry's office until granted an audience.

'Hi. I'm Ian Carroll. A playwright from Liverpool. I've flown here, especially. Yes, I can wait. I only need five minutes of his time.'

Then, when granted that five-minute audience, I would have said this.

'Please don't sack Dalglish. He hasn't managed in the Premiership for a long time, so you have to give him time to blow the cobwebs off. He's blooding these players, teaching them how to be winners, and he's already done that this season. Now that he's had a year to familiarise himself with the opposition, many of this year's draws will be wins next season. No one is calling for his head. Everyone is behind him. You don't need to make a change. Just sit back and watch us win.'

You never know, it might have worked.

Instead, I never made the roundtrip to Boston, and John W Henry sacked Dalglish.

I was gutted.

Most Liverpool fans were.

Especially when you consider that he sacked King Kenny for nothing, and for no-one. The owner didn't even have a replacement lined up.

FSG approached former Everton boss Roberto Martinez about taking over, but he declined. They then ended up focussing on Brendan Rodgers, formerly of Swansea.

These were both decent blokes, but what was wrong with Kenny? He was better by a country mile. Even Tom Werner had stated, only a few months earlier, tell me a coach anywhere in the world more loved by his supporters than Kenny Dalglish?

The answer was, there wasn't one.

Craig Bellamy left the club in the close season.

In his autobiography, he said, 'When the owners decided to sack Dalglish, who had just delivered the club's first trophy in six years, I knew that it was time to go.'

But despite the disappointment (by which I mean devastation) that greeted the announcement, we supporters can't just jump ship. We're Liverpool fans first.

Brendan Rodgers was eventually announced as our new manager.

I was underwhelmed, to say the least.

CHAPTER THIRTY-SIX

Brendan Rodgers announced his vision for the style of football that he wanted the Liverpool team to play.

He wanted a high press, to win the ball back from the opposition within six seconds of them having the ball, to have more possession, and use the Tiki-taka system – like Barcelona – with short passes and zonal movement rather than playing a formal system.

I thought, that all sounds wonderful. And what is the other team going to be doing while we're doing that? Sitting in the stands, applauding?

No doubt I was still hurting from the departure of Dalglish, but I was also sceptical about our new managerial appointment.

He had been a youth team coach at Chelsea, and then had managerial stints with Watford, Reading, and Swansea, with whom he gained promotion to the Premiership and – against all expectations – kept them in the top flight. He had done well with these so-called lesser teams. Could he work at the highest level of the game, where Liverpool wanted to be? He was only 39 years of age. Did he have the experience and the nous to match The Reds' ambition? He'd signed a three-year contract, and now he had the opportunity to show the club what he could do.

Fabio Borini and Joe Allen came in. Alberto Aquilani, Dirk Kuyt, Charlie Adam and Craig Bellamy departed, while Andy Carroll went to West Ham on loan.

Rodgers told Jordan Henderson that he was surplus to requirements. He wanted to swap him for Clint Dempsey of Fulham. Henderson, still under contract, said that he wasn't going anywhere. He would rather stay and fight for his place. And that's what he did.

The league season did not get off to a good start. We lost 3-0 to West Brom at The Hawthorns. The Baggies were now managed by Steve Clarke. If we couldn't even beat our former assistant manager's new team, what hope did we have?

It seemed like regression.

We then drew two of our next four matches, while suffering defeats at home to Arsenal and Man Utd which appeared to confirm the hypothesis.

At the end of September, almost six weeks after the season began, came our first ray of light with a 5-2 victory away at Norwich. Suarez scored a hat-trick for the second season running against The Canaries.

The BBC reported that Liverpool had 'passed and purred' their way to victory. Maybe Rodgers was onto something after all.

We lost just one of our next ten games, an away defeat at Spurs. We had only won four and drawn five of the games in that sequence so, despite becoming hard to beat, we obviously weren't clinical enough. We were tenth in the league mid-December.

We were hit and miss up to and including the Christmas period, with two wins and two defeats.

Suarez was scoring for fun, but we could only manage ninth place in the table at the end of the calendar year.

Reinforcements were needed, and boy did we get them!

In came Daniel Sturridge and Philippe Coutinho in the January transfer window. The former cost £12 million from Chelsea. The little Brazilian cost £8.5 million from Inter Milan. They would both do great things for The Reds.

The New Year began with a 3-0 home win against Sunderland. There was a double for Suarez and a first league goal for Raheem Sterling, aged just 18 years and 25 days at the time.

Sterling had been signed from QPR in 2010 for less than half a million. He had been given his debut in the senior team the previous March under Kenny Dalglish. He would prove to be an amazing talent. We would recoup our money more than a hundred-fold when he eventually decided to leave.

The second half of the season saw Liverpool lose just three times, but there were far too many games drawn to make much headway up the table.

Henderson was chipping in with the goals. His stubborn refusal to swap places with Clint Dempsey was now reaping dividends for The Reds. He made 30 league appearances in the season, almost half of those from the subs bench, and scored five and provided four assists.

Sturridge was also scoring freely, as was our captain and stalwart Steven Gerrard and, of course, Luis Suarez.

But, it was all to no avail.

We finished the campaign in seventh position. We had also limped tamely out of the cup competitions.

We ended up on 61 points. This was nine more than Dalglish had managed the previous year, but Kenny could claim to have been distracted by our run to the finals of both domestic cups.

Still, it was early days. We had to give the new manager time. And, at least there would be one less obstacle to face in the coming season as – having just won the league with Man Utd – Alex Ferguson announced his retirement.

After 27 years in charge of The Red Devils, and with 20 title wins now under their belts, compared to our 18, Fergie clearly felt he had done enough.

He handed the baton to David Moyes, the Everton manager. While he'd kept The Toffees in the Premiership throughout his 11-year tenure with the club, he had failed to win a single match away from home against the top four of Liverpool, Arsenal, Chelsea, and Man Utd. Then again, he'd only had 43 attempts!

How would Moyes handle the pressure of delivering week in and week out on a stage as big as Old Trafford? How would Man Utd cope without their usual man in the dug-out? Would it be a seamless transition, or were the wheels about to come off the Man Utd juggernaut?

We would soon find out, but one thing was sure. This represented a unique opportunity for Brendan Rodgers. Did he have what it takes?

Not judging by his transfer activity in the close season he didn't. Out went Andy Carroll and Stewart Downing. In came Iago Aspas and Mamadou Sakho. We also changed goalkeepers. Pepe Reina left for Napoli on a 12-month loan. In his place came Simon Mignolet for £9 million from Sunderland.

Still working in that same Warrington office at the time, I asked one of the Man Utd fans, who really knew his football (not easy to admit, giving the team that he supported) if Simon Mignolet was any good. I didn't really know much about him.

'He's not as good as Pepe Reina,' was all he said. Turned out he was right!

Would this be the season that we finally won the Premier League? I wasn't hopeful as the 2013/2014 campaign began.

But what a start we made.

Three wins out of three, each by a single goal to nil, and each of them by Daniel Sturridge. We had maximum points and were top of the league. The last of the three matches was particularly sweet as it was a victory over Man Utd at Anfield, and came on the 100th anniversary of the birth of Bill Shankly.

We were then brought down to earth with a draw away at Swansea before a home defeat to Southampton with future-Red Dejan Lovren getting the only goal of the game.

We won three of our next four matches, with Sturridge netting four times in that run and Suarez, having just returned from yet another suspension, scoring a total of six, including a hat-trick against West Brom.

A defeat to Arsenal was followed by a 4-0 thrashing of Fulham, before a pulsating 3-3 draw against neighbours Everton. Suarez and Sturridge were again on the scoresheet.

At the start of December, we lost away at Hull city before finding our best form of the season so far.

We beat Norwich City 5-1 at Anfield. Suarez bagged four of the goals, to top his hat-tricks against them in the previous two campaigns.

Then, with three more victories in quick succession, we were back on top of the table.

Suarez had grabbed a brace in each of those last three games. It meant he had scored ten times in just four matches.

On Christmas Day 2013, Liverpool looked down on the rest of the Premier League.

'Please Santa. All I want this year is for us to stay there.'

I should have asked for something else.

We lost twice in quick succession between Boxing Day and New Year to leave us in fifth position.

January brought three wins and a draw.

February started with a 1-1 draw away at West Brom.

We were now in fourth place in the league.

We then thrashed Arsenal 5-1 at Anfield. Sterling scored twice.

It appeared to be a real coming-of-age for the young forward. After each goal, he put his hand to his face in an unrehearsed celebration, as if to say 'Oh my God! What just happened? I really can do it at this level.' It was quite endearing. And what a prospect he was.

As I left the game, and made my way to the pub afterwards, I saw a TV crew interviewing elated Liverpool fans, trying to get a soundbite.

I had the urge to run up to them and shove my face in front of the camera, the way those idiot fans do (and I would be one of them), and shout 'Radio-Raheem!' – the quote coming from Spike Lee's cult-movie 'Do The Right Thing'.

I'm not sure how many people would have got it, but it summed up how I felt.

We then went on a run of ten straight victories, one of which was an away win at Old Trafford, where we won by an eye-popping three goals to nil.

We were in second place after the Man Utd result, four points behind leaders Chelsea, but with a game in hand.

Man City were two points behind us in third place, but they had played two games fewer than us and were still breathing down our necks.

Our winning streak continued as we dispatched Cardiff, Sunderland, Spurs, and West Ham, scoring 14 times in those four matches.

We were top of the league for what looked to be a title-decider when Man City came to Anfield with just five games of the season left to play.

And beat them we did, by three goals to two.

The Premier League trophy was ours for the taking. The future was in our own hands.

A hard-fought victory away at Norwich left us five points clear at the top of the league with only three matches still to play.

Chelsea were in second place.

Man City were nine points behind us, but they still had those two games in hand.

Two wins and a draw meant we would be champions, Premier League winners for the first time.

If City failed to win all of their remaining matches, we would need even fewer points to secure the crown.

Next up were Chelsea at Anfield.

We just needed a draw.

Mourinho though had other ideas. He's Niccolo Machiavelli reborn!

He knew the crowd would be raucous. He'd felt the force of our fans at our first Champions League meeting, when an early onslaught caught him and his team out and upset his carefully thought-out game-plan.

There would be no repeat this time.

The Kop would be singing. We'd want to get at them. Though we only needed a draw to leave the league still in our hands, we'd been scoring for fun of late so we would probably go for the win.

Jose knew all of that.

Within 30 seconds of the kick-off, the ball went back to Petr Cech in their goal.

He took a touch. And then another.

He didn't just launch it up-field.

The Anfield crowd were incensed. Chelsea were, my god, time-wasting!

We started booing.

Mourinho, the pantomime villain, must have been loving it.

His plan had worked.

Instead of cheering our team, we were booing theirs.

How clever is that? It is actually genius.

He had another trick up his sleeve too, old Mourinho.

No 90 minutes of play is ever complete without the other team getting at least one chance.

He planned to soak up our pressure and hit long balls up to Demba Ba, who was sure to get an opportunity at some point in the match.

And so it proved.

While the opposition defence and midfield worked hard in banks of four and five to stifle our advances, Liverpool sought to pass the ball around, probing for weaknesses in the Chelsea lines.

Steven Gerrard dropped deep to take possession and, inexplicably and horribly, the ball rolled under his foot and ran away from him.

As he turned and tried to recover, his feet went from under him.

Demba Ba ran onto the loose ball and closed in on the Liverpool goal, sliding the ball under Simon Mignolet and into the back of the net.

Hearts were being broken. A new Steven Gerrard song was born amongst away fans.

As we threw everything at Chelsea to try to get back into the game, they broke away again in the last minute. This time, it was the traitor Torres leading the charge. He squared the ball to Willian who tapped it into an empty net.

The match finished 2-0 to the Londoners.

We were still top of the league on 80 points, but Man City were on 77 points with a game in hand and a far superior goal difference.

The title was no longer in our own hands.

When City won their game in hand, against Everton no less (thanks, guys. I'm sure you gave it your all!), we dropped down to second in the league table.

We then drew one and won one in our last two games, while Man City won both of their matches.

They were champions on 86 points. We were runners up on 84 points.

We had run them so close. We had scored more top-flight goals than we ever had before in a single season. We had won precisely f*ck all.

I've previously said I wasn't pinning my hopes on Brendan Rodgers. When the team was doing well, and it looked like we might win the league, I did not change my tune.

I said, to all who would listen, that I hope that he makes me eat my words. Rams them down my throat, in fact. Please, please, please prove me wrong.

And he very nearly did.

Our last game of the season had been at home to Newcastle. We won by two goals to one. If City had lost their last match, we would have been champions. But they didn't.

Liverpool city centre was buzzing anyway; hoping against hope for a final day miracle.

When it didn't happen, we all still decided to party.

My wife and I were in a bar on Duke Street called the Sound Café.

There were music fans and football fans all crowded in together.

There was a German punk band all set to play.

They did their sound-check, and were about to launch into their first number.

But we wouldn't let them.

Everyone was dancing on the chairs and on the tables, singing and chanting and punching the air.

'We are Liverpool, la, la, la, la, la.

We are Liverpool, la, la, la, la, la.

We are Liverpool, la, la, la, la, la.

We're the best football team in the land.

Yes, we are.

Poetry in motion…'

Every time the band began to sing, we would drown them out.

Their female vocalist was gobsmacked.

Who are these guys (and gals)?

Why do they do this?

No one sings louder than a punk band.

Except we did.

And it was great.

Imagine what it would have been like if we had actually won something?

Roll on the next season.

Surely, we wouldn't have too much longer to wait.

We'd *almost* won the Premier League.

Could we go again?

CHAPTER THIRTY-SEVEN

For the 2014/2015 season, hopes were high that Liverpool could now compete with the very best. Brendan Rodgers had proved that he had what it takes to manage a top team in the Premiership. Could he now deliver the trophy that the fans wanted most?

His task was not made any easier with the departure of Luis Suarez, our leading goal-scorer for the last three years, who moved to Barcelona for a fee of £65 million.

Coming in the opposite direction were Liverpool-fan Rickie Lambert, Adam Lallana, and Dejan Lovren, all from Southampton. We could have saved almost £50 million in transfer fees if we had just changed our club name from ours to theirs!

We also bought midfielder Emre Can and Divock Origi to play up front. Most surprising of all was our purchase of Mario Balotelli for £16 million from AC Milan.

Jose Mourinho had previously worked with Balotelli and simply described him as 'uncoachable'. He wasn't wrong.

I was particularly pleased with the arrival of Origi, though. I remembered him from the 2014 World Cup where he had played for Belgium.

Though he was only a teenager at the time, the crowd in the stadium would get to their feet whenever he got on the ball. He was the only player I saw them do this for throughout the entire tournament. And this for an 18-year-old. In Brazil.

I hoped that Liverpool supporters would give him time to show what he could do. I suppose, in a way, a few memorable moments aside, we're still waiting.

We had run Man City close the previous season. Chelsea too would be in the mix. Mourinho had returned to the London club after a successful spell abroad, though he had finished in third place in the Premiership last time out. He was keen to point out that he had beaten both of the teams that finished above him, us and City, both home and away.

Which was true.

For sure, with his first season back in charge under his belt, he would be a formidable adversary.

We would need to up our game to end our long wait for a Premier League title.

Would this be our year?

No. That's the simple answer.

Though we won our first game, we lost half of our opening dozen matches. We were 12th in the league.

We won two and drew one of our next three matches, before we lost 3-0 at Old Trafford to a United team managed by Louis Van Gaal.

Despite David Moyes being Alex Ferguson's personal choice to succeed him, and Fergie's request to the club and their fans that he be given time, Moyes had lasted just ten months in the job.

We then picked ourselves up to go 13 games undefeated, recording ten wins in that sequence to lift us up to fifth in the table.

That appeared to be the extent of our bluster, as we then lost our next two games. The first was a home game against Man Utd. Our recent run of form meant that we would leap-frog them in the table and go up to fourth with a win.

Steven Gerrard had been left on the bench. With United 1-0 up at half-time, Brendan Rodgers threw him into the fray.

Such was Gerrard's ire at not starting, and his desire to wrest control of the game back from our bitter rivals, that he flew into two tackles immediately after coming on. He was gone in just 38 seconds!

We lost the game 2-1, and then got turned over by Arsenal 4-1 at the Emirates.

We limped to the end of the season with two wins, two draws, and three defeats in our last seven matches, finishing sixth in the league.

Our last game of the campaign was a 6-1 defeat away at Stoke. Says it all, really.

We also went out of both the League Cup and the FA Cup at the semi-final stage, and the Champions League in the first group stage.

It wasn't progress. It was capitulation.

It seemed that we had reached our apogee under Brendan Rodgers during the previous season, but the owners – which you can't really fault them for – looked like sticking by their man.

Rodgers was allowed to prepare for the coming season.

Steven Gerrard, meanwhile, left for a final swansong at LA Galaxy. We waved a fond farewell to the Anfield icon and club legend. He had given his all for us. He was one hell of a player. The only thing missing from his Liverpool CV was the league title. You never know, maybe one day he'll come back and win it as manager. I'd like that.

Raheem Sterling moved to Man City for a fee that would rise to £49 million. Like in the case of Michael Owen, I'm sure he was a player who would have stayed if we had showed him a little more love from the terraces. But, as soon as he refused to sign the first contract offer that was placed in front of him, the fans seemed to turn against him.

If we had sung his name and shown him how much we thought of him, I'm sure he would have found agreement with the club – on terms that suited him – and that he would have stayed.

Instead, we went cold.

'Just sign the contract, you greedy bastard,' seemed to be the verdict.

We gave him every excuse to seek pastures new.

Also outgoing were Rickie Lambert and Fabio Borini.

Incoming were James Milner on a free transfer; an excellent signing. Also young Joe Gomez for £3.5 million from Charlton; again a thoroughly good buy.

Striker Danny Ings came in from Burnley. We also got Nathaniel Clyne from Southampton, who pocketed another £10 mill of our dough.

Our big-money purchase was Roberto Firmino from Hoffenheim. The Brazilian cost us £21 million. If they'd have asked for gold nuggets instead of pound coins, he'd still have been worth every penny.

We also bought Christian Benteke from Aston Villa for £32 million. Don't ask me why.

I'll re-phrase that, as I think I know why. He'd played well against us in the FA Cup semi-final at Wembley, the season before. He'd been a handful.

Rather than come up with a plan to nullify his physical presence in future matches, Rodgers decided to buy him instead.

It seemed to me to smack of desperation.

He was never a Liverpool player.

Still, it was Brendan's call and, as we entered the new season, he was still the man in charge.

Two wins and a draw, all to clean sheets, meant a not-too-bad start to the season.

Benteke scored the winner at home against Southampton. Maybe he would prove me wrong after all, as Rodgers had almost done the season before.

But it still didn't whisper 'excitement'. It didn't state that we were back where we belonged.

There was still no hope that our wait for a Premier League title was coming to an end anytime soon.

Then we lost 3-0 at home to West Ham, their first victory at Anfield since 1963 when Bobby Moore was playing for them.

We subsequently went to Old Trafford and were roundly defeated by three goals to one. To be fair, Benteke scored his second of the season. Credit where it is due.

We drew against Norwich, beat Aston villa, and then went to Goodison Park.

The game ended one apiece and, sensing that this ship had run aground, the owners sacked Brendan Rodgers an hour after the match.

It was the 4th of October, 2015. The decision to replace him had already been taken. Had he won 10-0 (which would have been nice), he'd still have been sacked.

Rodgers released a statement saying that it had been an honour to manage one of the game's great clubs.

In his place came one of the game's emerging managers.

His name was Jurgen Klopp.

CHAPTER THIRTY-EIGHT

Jurgen Klopp took over as Liverpool manager in October 2015. At his first press conference in charge, he wowed reporters with his passion and articulation.

He began by saying that 25 years was a long time for the club to have gone without winning the league. It was clear where his focus was, and what he had been brought in to achieve.

He wanted to turn the fans from doubters to believers. He said he thought we could win the title within four years. He would also do it by playing interesting football.

So, no pressure then.

Klopp had been an average footballer himself. He had played 337 times for Mainz in Germany, scoring 50 goals as a forward before dropping back into defence.

He said 'I had the talent for the 5th division and the mind for the Bundesliga. The result was a career in the Second Division.'

He spent a total of 18 years with the club as both player and manager. After a couple of near-misses, he finally got the club into the Bundesliga for the first time in their history. They were later relegated and, when they missed out on promotion by two points the following season, Klopp decided that it was time to go and said an emotional farewell to the fans.

Next stop was Borussia Dortmund. He was hired by the Dortmund CEO Hans Joachim Watzke. He had been an admirer having played against Klopp's previous team.

'They always seemed to have more players on the pitch than you did,' Watzke said. He wondered how their coach had managed to inspire such endeavour. Now he had the chance to find out for himself, and the result was two Bundesliga titles in the seven years that Klopp was there.

Again, when Klopp felt that he had taken the club as far as he could, he moved on, parting on the very best of terms.

After a four-month sabbatical, he had accepted the Liverpool job. When it was offered to him, he had phoned Didi Hamann to ask him if he thought he should take it on.

Hamann had no hesitation and announced that Liverpool would be perfect for Klopp. Klopp would also be perfect for Liverpool.

The new German manager did not promise miracles. He said that we would work hard, run more, and try to pick up points. He wanted us to ooze vitality. He wanted us to be the hardest team in the world to beat.

His first match in charge was a scoreless draw away to Spurs at White Hart Lane. Liverpool ran more than they had in any previous league game that season. In fact, they ran more than *any* team had run in the league. Klopp was certainly being listened to by his players.

The team showed plenty of the intense pressing that their new manager wanted to see. Clearly inspired by Klopp, Liverpool battled hard for their point that day and registered their first clean sheet of the season.

Klopp stood on the touchline, punching the air in celebration after each sprint, tackle, shot, and save.

At the end of the match, he strolled onto the pitch, an act that is now hugely recognisable, and hugged each of his players.

You might have thought the team had actually won something.

In a post-match interview, Klopp said '0-0 is not my dream result, but it is okay. I am happy because I saw many good things. In the first 20 minutes, we were pressing and were very aggressive. We will get stronger.'

He continued, 'There were many full-throttle moments in the game. We need to improve but, after working with the players for three days, I am completely satisfied.'

On the future as a whole, Jurgen had this to say.

'We will play good football on the good days. On the less good days, we will fight for the result. I'm really optimistic for the future. Not because I am crazy but because I know what we have, I know what we can get, and I know that we have a really super bunch of people: knowledge, character, not just the players, but all around.'

A week later came Klopp's first game at home in the league. Southampton provided the opposition.

Benteke put Liverpool ahead in the 77th minute before The Saints levelled with just four minutes to go. The scorer of Southampton's goal was Sadio Mane. Their defence was marshalled by Virgil van Dijk.

Klopp had previously failed to sign Mane for Borussia Dortmund. It was a decision that he said he had come to regret. Or, in Jurgen-speak, he said 'I wanted to punch myself for not signing him!'

Next up came a tough away game at Chelsea.

We fell behind to an early goal by Ramires, but Klopp had turned his doubters into believers and Liverpool kept going.

The Reds equalised on the stroke of half-time, Bobby Firmino setting up fellow-Brazilian Coutinho for the goal.

Liverpool scored two more in the second half to run out 3-1 winners. It was Klopp's first league win in charge.

We had played in the manner that the manager desired and had simply outrun and outfought Chelsea.

According to media reports, Klopp was an animated figure on the touchline, not just in encouraging his players, but also delivering the most fearful verbal volleys when someone did not do as he demanded.

It also proved to be Jose Mourinho's last match in charge of Chelsea. He had cut a forlorn figure in his technical area, largely slumped in his seat while Klopp was urging his players on to victory. I guess he knew what was coming.

Next up was a home game against Crystal Palace which we might have been expected to win. But, a 5,000-mile roundtrip to Russian side Rubin Kazan just three days earlier did not do The Reds any favours.

The Palace manager, Alan Pardew, long a bogey-man for us, was determined to come out of the blocks smartly to try and take advantage of any lethargy in Liverpool's legs.

It worked, and Klopp suffered his first loss in the seven matches that he had been in charge of The Reds for, across all competitions.

Many supporters heading for the exits before the final whistle had sounded, and Klopp later berated those who left early by saying that they had let him walk alone. We had abandoned him to his fate as the team tasted defeat.

It would not happen again. The crowd were right behind him after that. He made it clear to us all that this was a mission and, if we wanted him to succeed, then we had better be there by his side.

Next up was a tough away game at title-favourites Manchester City. The result was a rousing 4-1 victory for The Reds, with a goal and an assist from each of Bobby Firmino and Philippe Coutinho.

The two Brazilians were starting to flourish under Klopp. Firmino was being played in a more advanced position, and was preferred up front to Christian Benteke.

While City didn't know what had hit them, Klopp said, 'We played with big passion, and that's the most important thing for us. The good news is that we can do better.'

The papers reported that all of the signs of what the former Borussia Dortmund coach wanted from his team were on display in this game. City couldn't get out of their own half as Liverpool constantly went in search of the ball. The City supporters turned on their own team as Liverpool cut through City's defence at will, with Klopp urging his players not to take a backward step as they went in search of what would be a highly impressive victory.

When James Milner scored the only goal, from the penalty spot, of our next match at home to Swansea, Liverpool moved up to sixth place in the league.

It seemed like we were making progress. There was cause for optimism and, not only that, there seemed to be a real belief – from both players and fans – in Klopp's philosophy and style of play.

We were getting more bang for our buck. Our players were running more, fighting more for the ball, taking more shots, seeking more possession. We played with *purpose*. We had a *plan*.

It was still early days, but it felt – well – good.

If I couldn't have King Kenny back, I would settle for Jurgen. I believed.

Little did we know that sixth would be the highest position we would achieve in the league that season. There would be no more upward trajectory in that competition.

In the cups, however, we were really flexing our muscles. We made it to the League Cup final, where we were up against Man City at Wembley.

The 90 minutes ended in a 1-1 draw, a result which remained unchanged at the end of extra-time.

In the penalty shoot-out, Emre Can scored our first, while City missed theirs.

It looked like Klopp might celebrate his first season in charge, and not even a full season at that, with a first trophy for The Reds.

Then, Liverpool managed to miss their next three spot-kicks, while City scored all three of theirs.

It was disappointing. It would have been affirmation that we really did have the right man in the dug-out. But, Klopp had lost his first final in charge of The Reds.

Still, we had also made it to the Europa League final, where we would face Sevilla in Basel, Switzerland.

We'd had an interesting run to the final, beating Manchester United in a two-legged tie to confirm our superior European pedigree.

In the quarter-finals, we had faced Klopp's old Dortmund team. After a 1-1 draw away in the first leg, Borussia came to Anfield and played their part in an amazing night.

What happens when two Klopp teams go head-to-head?

The result is 'Boom!'

Within ten minutes of the kick-off, we were 2-0 down. Because of the away-goals rule, we would need to score three without reply in order to win.

Origi pulled one back early in the second half to raise hopes of another great European night at Anfield.

We'd had so many down the years, we all felt that anything was possible.

Then Dortmund scored again, and that seemed to put an end to such ideas.

There were 25 minutes left on the clock, and we still needed to score three times.

On 66 minutes, up popped Coutinho to claw one back.

On 78 minutes, Sakho got an unlikely goal to leave us needing just one more.

Then, in injury time and with just seconds remaining, Dejan Lovren smashed a header into the Kop-end goal.

We had done it again!

Interviewed after the game, and asked to give his thoughts on what he had just witnessed, Klopp answered simply 'Boom!'

He called it 'Heavy-Metal football'.

He wasn't far wrong.

It was certainly exciting, and also unpredictable. It also looked like it might produce results as we then overcame Villarreal in the semi to take our place in the final.

Sevilla had won the Europa League in each of the two previous seasons. They had to be favourites, but we were Liverpool, and this was a European competition. We had proved in the past that anything was possible.

For the first 45 minutes in the final, we were the better team. We had taken a 1-0 lead into the interval courtesy of a Daniel Sturridge goal.

We were faster to the ball than the Spanish side; they seemed to have run out of ideas.

We had crushed the spirit out of them.

It felt like it was going to be our night.

Sevilla would probably have a go at us early in the second half before they accepted the inevitable. All we had to do was see out that early onslaught and that would surely be the extent of Sevilla's challenge.

Just extinguish that last glimmer of hope before… oh, shit. They scored early in the second half.

The game had only just kicked off again when the Spanish team equalised. There were just 17 seconds gone when they scored.

Alberto Moreno made a poor headed clearance and the ball fell to a Sevilla forward, who then raced up to and past Moreno and crossed for a simple tap-in for Kevin Gameiro. Twice Moreno had had the opportunity to clear it. It felt like we had gifted them an opportunity to get back in the game.

Two further second-half goals saw Sevilla lift the cup.

We'd finished eighth in the league, and runners-up in two cup competitions.

Was Klopp just unlucky?

Were the fans unfair to expect our new manager to lift silverware in his first season with the club?

All of his inspired rhetoric had raised expectations amongst supporters. He had asked us to believe, and we had, and we did.

As Leicester City went on to become the unlikeliest winners of the Premier League that year, Klopp must have thought that anything was possible. Having only arrived the previous October. He'd not even had a full season in charge yet.

That was about to change, though, as we got ready for 2016/2017.

CHAPTER THIRTY-NINE

This was the club's 125th year of existence. It was our 25th consecutive year in the Premier League. It was 26 years since we had been champions. It was Klopp's first full season in charge.

Out went Joe Allen, Mario Balotelli, and Christian Benteke, the latter to Crystal Palace for a significant sum which allowed us to recover a large part of his initial transfer fee.

In came Sadio Mane and Georginio Wijnaldum, from Southampton and Newcastle respectively.

Mane held the record for scoring the fastest hat-trick in the Premiership. Robbie Fowler had previously held the record when netting three against Arsenal in just over four minutes. Sadio scored his three in less than three minutes!

We had lost Raheem Sterling to Man City the season before, and I was gutted to see him go. Mane looked like being Sterling's replacement. I liked Mane, but I didn't think he was half the player that Sterling was. I'm pleased to say that I was proved wrong, and then some. I now think, in 2020, that Mane is probably the best player in the world. He's certainly the best player in Britain.

A lot more players left the club than came in. It seemed that Klopp wanted a slightly-trimmed squad, though one with more quality. We actually had more money coming in than going out in the close-season transfer business.

One pre-season match ended with Liverpool beating Barcelona 4-0 at Wembley. That's a scoreline that we would replicate, to great effect, just a few short years later.

The Liverpool side were described as having run riot. It was a sign that we could compete with, and defeat, the very best.

The league season began with a trip to The Emirates. The game was 1-1 at half time before a stunning Liverpool performance in the second half, in what was a thrilling game, saw The Reds emerge as 4-3 winners.

It was exciting stuff.

A trip to Turf Moor followed, and we were brought down to earth by a dogged Burnley side. They beat us 2-0 thanks to two first-half goals.

The result wasn't entirely unexpected. It was becoming known as one of the toughest grounds in the country to get a result.

We'd have to take our medicine and move on.

We did this in style, winning eight and drawing three of our next 11 matches.

We were second in the league. Not only that, we were scoring goals for fun.

We were becoming the nation's second-favourite team for our free-flowing football.

Next came an away trip to Bournemouth. I have family in the town, so we always try to make the trip. We used to go down there whenever we played Portsmouth or Southampton. Now, The Cherries themselves were in the Premiership, which made things even better. We could walk to the ground from my aunt and uncle's house.

We were 2-0 up at half time and looked on course for victory.

When they scored early in the second half, we quickly got another to maintain our two-goal advantage.

Then, in a frantic last 15 minutes, Bournemouth netted three times!

Reds fans were shell-shocked.

Cherries-supporters serenaded us with a rousing rendition of '3-1 and you f*cked it up. 3-1 and you f*cked it up,' etc. etc.

It was right, but it wasn't fun. We'd been beaten by four goals to three.

We ended the calendar year with four straight wins, the last of which was a 1-0 victory over Manchester City at Anfield, the goal coming via a Wijnaldum header.

I felt a little sorry for the Dutch midfielder. I thought he was a great player, but he hadn't been given a proper run in the side. Despite having scored the winner, he was dropped for the next match. You can't expect someone to show consistency if they're playing one week and not the next. Still, I was sure his time would come.

The match against Man City represented a first meeting in English football between Klopp and Pep Guardiola. They had a record of four wins each from eight previous matches on German soil, when Pep's Bayern Munich had taken on Jurgen's Dortmund team.

Guardiola was considered the world's best footballing coach, but even he had been left in awe of Klopp's work at Borussia Dortmund.

After one meeting, Guardiola said post-match, 'They are like a steamroller. Unstoppable. I've never seen anything like it. They are completely focussed for 90 minutes, waiting for you to mess up a pass so that they can set their sprinters on you.' He then added, reflectively, 'I must take some time to really study this and see if there's a way to stop them.'

It was high praise indeed, but that was Klopp's way. He wanted everything played at full speed, Everything happening at full-throttle. He wanted to do everything fast and precisely, to try to find the shortest route to the opposition defence.

Despite the victory over Man City, Chelsea – under new manager Antonio Conte – were six points clear at the top of the league and were proving difficult to haul in.

January and February produced mixed results and saw The Reds defeated three times.

We then recovered and would lose just one more game between March and the end of the season.

Chelsea were crowned champions. We came in fourth.

Phil Coutinho and Sadio Mane were our joint top-scorers in the league with 13 apiece. Firmino was just behind them on 11.

We were sharing the goals, and sharing the love.

Despite going out of the FA Cup early, and losing in the semi-finals of the League Cup, there were plenty of positives to take from the season.

We were playing attractive football. We had shown that we were capable of putting a decent run of results together.

Could we keep that up over the course of a full campaign, though?

Time would tell.

We still looked a little shaky at the back. I don't think anyone thought that Mignolet was good enough in goal, while the back-up keeper Loris Karius was a bit of an unknown quantity.

We had unearthed a gem at right-back, however, with the promotion of Trent Alexander-Arnold to the first team. The locally-born lad had already put in some eye-catching performances in his first season in the Premiership. His stated ambition was not just to play for the club but to one day be captain.

I'm sure that he'll get there, and I'm convinced that – by the time he hangs up his boots, many years in the future – he will be held in the same esteem as Steven Gerrard. Which is saying a lot.

In fact, depending on the number of medals he acquires in his career, he may even surpass the great man himself. That would be quite something. He is truly a young man with the world at his feet. I love watching him play, and he will only get better.

Trent Alexander-Arnold, the Scouser in our team.

Coming into the team in time for the start of the new season was Mohamed Salah, bought from Roma for £36 million.

He'd had one previous spell in English football when he'd joined Chelsea at the age of 21. It hadn't worked out too well for him at the time, and he only spent a year with the London club before being sent out to Italy on loan before later signing permanently for Roma.

With a good season in Serie A under his belt, Liverpool came in for him.

Salah was pleased to get a second chance in the Premiership. He felt like he hadn't shown what he was capable of the first time around. He had unfinished business.

He'd grown up and matured into a better player.

Everyone was about to find out just how good the Egyptian was, as he took English football by storm.

CHAPTER FORTY

The 2017/2018 season began with a 3-3 draw away at Watford. Salah, Mane, and Firmino all scored. It was a sign of things to come.

Together with Philippe Coutinho, playing in behind the front three and pulling the strings, they would soon become known as The Fab Four, a title that they richly deserved.

They were beautiful to watch, and horrible to play against.

We won our next two matches, the last of which was a 4-0 defeat of Arsenal at Anfield, with our three forwards each on the scoresheet again.

The omens were good when we travelled to title-favourites Manchester City at the Etihad.

This would be a test of our true credentials.

An early Aguero goal put a slight dent in our aspirations, and then a harsh sending off for Mane after 37 minutes put an end to the game as a contest.

Chasing a long through-ball, Sadio had every right to go for it. The City goalie came rushing out of his area and headed the ball as Mane tried to reach it with a high boot.

It was a nasty collision, and I felt sorry for the keeper, but there was no intent on Mane's part and he was entitled to try and reach it.

It could have been a yellow, at most, for dangerous play, but it certainly didn't deserve a red card. I'm biased, obviously, but I still thought (and still think) that it was harsh.

We were eventually trounced by five goals to nil. This wasn't as bad as it sounds when you consider we had played a magnificent City side for an hour with ten men. It was difficult enough with 11 men on the pitch, and the game might have ended differently had we been allowed to play with our full complement of players.

We recovered from this setback to lose just one of our next 19 matches as we rose up to third in the table.

The last victory in the sequence was a game against Man City, who were threatening to run away with the league.

It was a tense affair at Anfield. I'd managed to bag a pair of tickets in the Anfield Road section. I went with my mate, Colin. He doesn't go to many games; he probably gets to one game in every season.

He chose well for this one as it turned out to be a cracker.

We took an early lead through a brilliant strike by another new signing Alex Oxlade-Chamberlain.

I was always a fan of 'The Ox' and thought he was a good acquisition.

Then, Leroy Sane equalised just before half-time to remind everyone (as if we didn't know) how tough an opponent this City team were.

But someone must have forgotten to tell Bobby Firmino, as he impudently robbed John Stones of the ball and then cheekily lofted it over Ederson's head and into the corner of the net. It was as if he was saying, 'This is our ground, and we'll win if we want to!'

He got a yellow card for removing his shirt as he celebrated the goal.

Then Mane hit the post, before scoring with his next attempt, barely three minutes after Bobby had put us ahead.

Seven minutes later, Salah scored from 35 yards after Ederson had come a long way out of his goal to attempt a clearance, gifting the ball to Salah instead.

Cue further celebration.

Better still, the goals had all happened at the end of the ground where I was sitting, so I got a great view of all three as we scored in quick succession. It was a crazy nine minutes and put us 4-1 up. Though we knew we'd never catch City in the league, it was still great to show them what we could do.

They then put two past us to give us a late scare, but the match ended up 4-3 to us. It was a marker, if not for this season, then certainly for the next.

There were eight wins, four draws, and just three defeats between that victory over Man City and the end of our league campaign.

Mohamed Salah ended up as our top-scorer with a remarkable 44 goals in all competitions with 32 of them in the Premier League.

In the January transfer window, we sold Philippe Coutinho to Barcelona for £105 million. Though we didn't want to sell him, the player wanted to go, so we had little choice. We did bring in Virgil van Dijk so, ultimately, we can be said to have put the money to good use.

While we finished in fourth place in the league, our season wasn't over.

We were off to Kiev for the small matter of a Champions League final against Real Madrid.

After topping our group in the first group stage, we had then trounced Porto 5-0 in the first knockout game, with goals again coming from Mane (hat-trick), Salah, and Firmino.

We then faced our domestic rivals Man City in the quarter-finals. While they were on their way to a Premier League title, they were no match for us in Europe as we beat them both home and away to end up with a 5-1 aggregate victory over the two legs.

The semi-finals were an amazing two games against Roma. I was on the kop to watch the first of those matches, where we raced to an unbelievable 5-0 lead before Roma clawed two back late on to give them a slender chance in the return game.

Salah, Mane, and Firmino again all scored. In fact, they scored all five.

In Rome, we took a 2-1 lead into the half-time interval and appeared to have one foot in the final. Three second-half goals for Roma gave the tie an incredible 7-6 aggregate score. Luckily, it was Liverpool who edged it, and we were heading for a European Cup final again.

Unfortunately, we were up against a wizened Real Madrid team with a pantomime villain in Sergei Ramos in the side. He would stop at nothing to see Madrid emerge as winners. His catalogue of misdemeanours in the final alone was more than some players notch up in their entire careers.

Liverpool started well. After a nervy first five minutes, we found our feet and began to probe the Madrid back-line, looking to impose our own style of play on the game.

Then, with Salah running with the ball about 30 yards from goal, and Ramos running alongside him, the Spaniard trapped Salah's arm in a grip before he fell over. With Salah pinned beneath him, Ramos rolled over and dislocated Salah's shoulder. It was a move straight out of a wrestling match.

Salah was forced off injured. We had lost one of our most potent and lightning-quick players.

At half time, the score was 0-0, but we had lost a little in the way of creativity and something in the way of belief when Salah was forced off injured. It would have been nice to see what we could have done with our best eleven on the pitch.

In the 49th minute of the match, Sergio Ramos runs into our box in support of an attack. Van Dijk gets ahead of Ramos' run and makes sure he can't get on the end of the Madrid cross. Unable to reach the ball, Ramos instead veers towards the Liverpool goalie Loris Karius and forearm smashes him in the face.

Had VAR been in use at the time, it would have been a straight red card. No question.

Or, had Karius simply stayed down on the ground where Ramos had put him, the officials would probably have figured out what had happened and would have sent Ramos off.

Instead, Karius groggily got back to his feet and complained to the referee, who allowed him to play on.

Two minutes later, Karius attempted to throw the ball out to one of our defenders and Karim Benzema, standing just two yards away but somehow unseen by the keeper, intercepted the throw and diverted the ball into the Liverpool net.

It was a cruel blow, and one made worse by the fact that Sergei Ramos' assault on our goalie had played no small part.

Four days after the final, Jurgen Klopp got a call from Franz Beckenbauer in Germany, who told him he had just been to visit the most famous doctor in that country. Beckenbauer said that the doctor had told him that Liverpool's goalie had suffered a concussion. That's what had led to him making his mistake.

The next day, Liverpool had Karius checked out. Even five days on from the final, he was still exhibiting 26 of the 30 medical markers that indicate a concussion.

Back in the final, Sadio Mane equalised for The Reds, but substitute Gareth Bale came on and changed the game. Within three minutes of coming off the bench, he had scored a wonderful overhead kick. Then, with seven minutes of the match remaining, a speculative long-range effort was let slip by the still-suffering Karius in the Liverpool goal.

The game ended 3-1 to Madrid.

In the words of Brian Clough, 'You've won nothing you cheating b*stards!'

The season ended empty-handed.

We'd now lost three cup finals under Jurgen Klopp.

We had also finished 25 points behind Man City in the league.

There was an awful lot of ground to make up.

Did we have what it took to bridge the gap?

Did we have the right man in charge to take us forward?

A new campaign was about to begin. It would turn out to be a cracker.

CHAPTER FORTY-ONE

It was clear we needed a new goalie. In came Alisson Becker from Roma for a world-record fee of £67 million. The record would be broken within a week, however, when Chelsea splashed out more for a keeper called Kepa. As they would try to offload him less than two years later, I think we certainly got the better deal.

Despite having conceded seven times against us in two games in the previous year's Champions League, Alisson would prove to be an amazing goalkeeper. Probably the best in the world.

We also brought in Naby Keita in midfield. Despite a slow start to his Anfield career, he is one that I wouldn't want to see leave. I believe he will come good.

Also incoming was Fabinho, a holding midfielder who plays in Brazil's defence and who we purchased from Monaco. He was another excellent acquisition.

Andy Robertson had come from Hull the season before for £8 million. It took a couple of months for him to break into the side but, as soon as he did, he went from strength to strength and never looked back.

He really came of age in the Champions League game against Man City when, crossing the halfway line from his left-back berth, he chased down three defenders, plus their goalie, and then their left-back before finally conceding a foul.

This one man was harassing half of City's team! Awesome. Simply awesome.

If Klopp's ambition was to entertain the crowd, this was exactly the sort of play, and the sort of player, to do just that.

This wasn't just Gegenpressing. This was Gegenpressing, and pressing, and pressing again!

The team had been improving under Klopp. We had been to three cup finals, although we had lost them all. We were more or less the only side in the land that could cope with – and come out on top over – Man City, despite their superior spend.

When our defence had been lacking, we bought van Dijk. When we needed a better goalie, we bought Becker.

I can remember when I lived in my old flat, and I had access to LFC TV. This was around 2010.

Our team was poor. The only player of any real quality was Steven Gerrard. In one match at home, we conceded a goal against a side we were expected to beat. The goal that we let in was sloppy, and scored late on. One of the papers the next day asked, 'Does he have to play in goal as well now?' We were a one-man team. Gerrard was carrying the club on his shoulders.

The LFC TV channel would show matches from previous seasons, and I would watch old games from 2001 to 2003 and almost weep for the quality that we had on display. Up front were Fowler, Heskey, Owen, and Anelka. In midfield were Hamann, McAllister, Berger, Smicer, and Murphy.

Now we had one man carrying the can.

Under Klopp, though, we were getting stronger, and plugging the gaps every season in those places where we could improve.

Still, I did hear rumblings of discontent. Not everyone thought he was the answer.

I still believed, however. I thought that this was a man with a plan.

We had 25 points to make up on Man City in the league from the season before. A tall order, but a new campaign was about to get underway.

Would our Champions League final defeat take the wind out of our sails, or would the injustice of it all fire us on to greater things?

Luckily, it was the latter, as the 2018/2019 season began with six straight wins to put us on top of the league.

We almost lost the next game, away to Chelsea, before a stunning last-minute goal from Daniel Sturridge levelled the tie.

A nervy 0-0 draw then followed against our title rivals Man City at Anfield. Riyad Mahrez missed a late penalty for the visitors, blazing his shot unforgivably over the bar.

It was a close escape, but the two consecutive draws moved us down to third place in the table.

We then won 11 and drew just once in our next dozen matches, which took us up to the end of the calendar year.

We were in top spot in the league, seven points clear of City having played the same number of games.

Next up was a trip to the Etihad. Win there, and we could really start to dream. Except we didn't. We lost 2-1 in a closely-fought match.

Dejan Lovren played Raheem Sterling onside, by just a fraction, and our former striker carried the ball forward before crossing for Leroy Sane to drill a pinpoint shot into the corner of our net.

The tension between both managers on the touchline, Klopp and Guardiola, was palpable. They knew this was almost a title decider. If we won, we'd be ten points clear. Lose, and there would be just four points separating the sides with 17 matches to play.

At the end of January, Liverpool played Leicester City at Anfield, whilst Man City had been beaten 2-1 by Newcastle the night before. If we were to win, we would open up a seven-point lead at the top of the table.

My wife and I had gone for a three-day break on the Isle of Man. It was freezing.

We headed out into the snow-filled streets to find a bar that was showing the match, and we found one on the sea-front. It was chocker. We managed to find a seat where, by straining our necks, we could just about catch the TV screen.

Liverpool went 1-0 up and appeared to be cruising but, just on the stroke of half-time, Andy Robertson committed a needless foul (Wijnaldum had him covered, so he had no need to jump in).

From the resulting free-kick, Harry Maguire scored for Leicester and the game eventually ended up 1-1.

We drew our next game against West Ham and lost top spot to Man City. Although we still had a game in hand, City would go the remainder of the season unbeaten, winning all of their matches.

Two further draws for ourselves meant we'd lost top spot and would never regain it.

We finished runners-up on 97 points. City were champions with 98.

We'd won our last nine matches, but by that time, the title was in City's hands. I felt that we'd bottled it.

I remember when Jose Mourinho won his first title with Chelsea back in 2005. They'd come out of the starting blocks on fire. They were early favourites for the title.

Gary Neville, trying to exert a bit of pressure, said that the Londoners would have to handle the expectation that came with being out in front.

Mourinho responded by saying that pressure was being in second place, knowing that you couldn't affect the outcome. Someone else's results would decide where you finished.

The following season, when Man Utd were top and Chelsea were in second, Mourinho was given the opportunity to say 'Man Utd have to prove they can handle the pressure'.

I thought that the Chelsea manager would do just that but, instead, he reiterated what he had said the season before. 'Pressure is not on the first place, who finish where they finish by their own results. Pressure is on the second. No matter what they do, the future is not theirs to decide.'

Whatever you think about Mourinho, he can't be labelled a hypocrite.

I thought we had only reached our maximum once we had given up pole position. I was disappointed. We'd had a great opportunity to end our long wait to win the Premier League.

In any other year, our points tally would have seen us comfortably over the line in first place.

Yet still, the wait went on.

We did, though, have the consolation(!) of another Champions League final.

And what a story that was.

CHAPTER FORTY-TWO

A tough Champions League group saw us drawn against Napoli, Red Star Belgrade, and the might of Paris St-Germain, featuring Neymar, Edinson Cavani, and Kylian Mbappe.

We scraped through in second place to face Bayern Munich in the first knockout stage.

We drew 0-0 in the first leg at Anfield before facing the Germans on home soil for the return match at the magnificent Allianz Arena.

Sadio Mane scored an early wonder goal to set us up for a 3-1 victory. To see him twist a goalkeeper of Manuel Neuer's calibre inside and out was simply remarkable.

At this point, I knew that anything was possible.

In the quarter-finals, we beat Porto both home and away. They must just sigh every time they get drawn against us. Always the bridesmaid and never the bride.

In the semi-finals, we were to face the Barcelona team of Lionel Messi and Luis Suarez.

We were nobody's favourites to win.

I was on holiday in Malta for the first leg, away at the Nou Camp.

I watched the match in the hotel bar. It didn't make for pretty viewing as we lost 3-0.

For the return leg at Anfield, I had a ticket for the match, but very little hope.

Just goes to show what I know.

We attacked early. Mane intercepted a back pass, squared it to Jordan Henderson, whose shot produced a save from ter Stegen in the Barca goal.

The keeper could only parry the ball into Origi's path, and the Belgian forward coolly slotted home.

We were 1-0 up after seven minutes.

We were without two of our first-choice front three for the match, with both Firmino and Mo Salah missing through injury, so no-one expected too much. Still, this was Anfield. This was Europe. We could dream.

In the second-half, Wijnaldum replaced Andy Robertson.

After 54 minutes, Trent Alexander-Arnold lost the ball.

Instead of tracking back, as you would expect a defender to do, he went hunting, closing down a Barcelona player and winning the ball back before carrying it upfield and crossing for Wijnaldum to sweep a shot into the back of the net.

We were two-nil to the good.

Just ten minutes later, Xherdan Shaqiri swung a cross in from the left-wing and Gini leapt head and shoulders above everyone to power the ball into the back of the net.

It was pandemonium. I was in the top tier of the main stand. I could scarcely believe it.

Then, Trent improvised what must go down as one of the best bits of football in the history of the game.

We won a corner. Trent placed the ball down.

He was walking away, to gain ground for a run-up, when he suddenly decided to spook the ball into the box towards Origi, the only player we had forward, while the Barca team appeared to be napping.

Origi said he saw the Barcelona keeper and a defender at the near post, so he decided to hook the ball aft.

It floated into the Barca net, and we held out for an insanely memorable 4-0 win.

We were off to a Champions League final for the second year running.

This time, our opponents would be Tottenham Hotspur who had defeated Ajax of Amsterdam in a pulsating semi-final of their own.

The match would be played at Athletico Madrid's stadium in Spain. My dad and my sister went. I didn't have a ticket, and I couldn't justify the expense of travelling there without one.

I watched it at home with Lesley. My mum came round, I did a barbecue, and we invited a few friends along.

An early penalty, won by Mane and converted by Salah, helped soothe a few nerves.

Later on, as Spurs threw everything at us, Alisson Becker produced save after save to keep Tottenham at bay.

With less than ten minutes to go, Sadio Mane picked up a ball on the left-wing.

He travelled the width of the pitch with it, shielding it magnificently, putting his foot on it, then sprinting past Christian Eriksen in the Spurs midfield with the nonchalance of a man running rings around his five-year-old kid in his back garden.

It was a magnificent piece of play, oozing confidence, and it almost produced a goal. James Milner only just shot wide at the end of this blistering attack.

Then, with just three minutes to go, Divock Origi fired into the bottom corner of the Tottenham net.

We won 2-0.

I could have wept with joy.

The following day, the team came home with the cup.

They would tour the city, starting at Allerton Maze, just 100 yards from my home.

My family and I went down to the end of the road to watch the arrival of the Liverpool team bus, and the small matter of them displaying the cup of my dreams.

It was joyous, simply joyous to see them drive up the avenue, bedecked in red and glory, sharing the moment with the fans.

We raised our flags and scarves and hailed our heroes. Tears were shed. Songs were sung.

We'd lost three cup finals in a row. We'd missed out on the league title by a point. I hate to think how despondent we might have been had we lost in Madrid.

Instead, I believe it inspired the players. I think it showed them how much the team meant to us, and how much their efforts, their skill, their talents, and teamwork meant to us.

I'm convinced they all thought 'I like this. I want more of this.'

Tom Werner, our Chairman, was aboard the bus. He turned to one of the directors and said 'I can't believe this. I've never seen anything like this.'

The response he received was, 'Oh, this is nothing. Just wait and see what it's like if we win the Premier League.'

Werner was dumbfounded, but the statement was true.

We had waited too long to win the trophy that we wanted most of all.

How much longer would we have to wait?

Well, the answer would come soon enough.

The 2019/2020 season was upon us.

It would prove to be the icing on the cake.

CHAPTER FORTY-THREE

There was little in the way of transfer business during the close season. Not much was needed. We were Champions of Europe. All of the pieces of the puzzle were in place for another tilt at the league title.

We began with a convincing home win against a plucky Norwich side. Though recently-promoted, they came to play football. At half-time, they were 4-0 down. The visitors clawed one back in the second half, but that was as good as it got for them.

I was in the Kenny Dalglish Stand, near the halfway line. It was a great seat to watch the opening match of the season. In fact, the season ticket I was using belonged to a friend of the family. It was the first time she ever lent it to us, and she said, 'Whatever you do, don't lose it. It was given to my dad by Bill Shankly himself.'

Apparently, they'd been neighbours, and Bill had chosen the seat especially. No wonder it was so good. It was directly opposite the directors' box in the main stand – what a glorious spot it was to see the new season get underway.

Todd Cantwell caught the eye for Norwich. I thought I was watching some Brazilian, but he's a terrific young English kid.

Liverpool were well-deserved victors on the day. We had our first three points on the board.

We'd also bagged our first trophy, pre-season, by beating Chelsea in the European Super Cup, played between the winners of the Champions League and Europa League.

It all augured well for the campaign ahead.

We won our first eight matches, then drew with Man Utd away with a late Lallana goal. Two more victories followed before an early title-showdown against Man City at Anfield.

We went into the game as league leaders, with City in second place.

After a 3-1 victory for The Reds, we were eight points clear at the top of the table, and nine points ahead of City, who dropped down to fourth place.

We then won our next 15 matches to open up a 22-point lead over Man City, who had climbed back up to second.

Liverpool fans were not only dreaming; we could actually start to think about lifting the trophy that we craved most of all. It would be our first

Premier League title, and the first time we had won the league in 30 years.

While we waited to be crowned title-winners, we had the comfort of knowing that, in Qatar in December, against Flamengo of Brazil, we had won the FIFA Club World Cup to be crowned the best football club in the world.

We were champions of Europe and champions of the world. Now, all we needed was to become champions of England as well.

After our recent run of success in the Premier League, we then lost 3-0 away to Watford before returning to winning ways away to Bournemouth.

We exited the Champions League on the 11th of March against Athletico Madrid, little realising it would be our last match for over three months due to the Covid pandemic.

When the season resumed in June, we were only six points away from winning the league.

We drew against Everton, and then thrashed Crystal Palace by four goals to nil.

The following night, Man City travelled to Chelsea. City needed to win all of their games even to have the slimmest of hopes of prolonging the title race.

On the 25th of June, Chelsea beat Man City 2-1.

It was all over. The Premier League title was ours.

I watched it on the TV and I cried.

Thirty years of waiting, of dreams and disappointment, all came to an end. A huge weight was lifted off the shoulders of every Liverpool fan.

Outside the house, I could hear the car horns beeping and the sound of fireworks exploding.

I grabbed my lucky LFC scarf. My wife put on my spare one.

We went down to the main road at the end of the street, just yards from where we'd watched our team parade the European Cup a summer earlier.

We joined our neighbours and sang and cheered and waved our scarves in the air, as every other car that passed us honked their horns in celebration.

It was glorious.

It was deserved.

We were Champions of England again!

CHAPTER FORTY-FOUR

We played out the rest of the season and ended up on 99 points. After our last home match of the campaign, a win against Chelsea, Jordan Henderson stood on a stage at Anfield and – to a backdrop of fireworks – lifted the Premier League trophy surrounded by his teammates.

Kenny Dalglish, who had brought Henderson to Liverpool nine years earlier, presented the winners' medals to Jordan and the rest of the players. No smile was bigger than The King's that night. No-one deserved to share in the celebrations more.

Behind the scenes, Jurgen Klopp had recently signed a new five-year contract extension. We hoped, and hope, that this is just the start.

The team had been unbeaten at Anfield for three seasons running. We were a force to be reckoned with.

Klopp had said, at his very first press conference at the club, that we would work hard and collect points. That was the goal.

We had amassed 196 of them in the last two seasons alone.

Each and every player had bought into Klopp's philosophy.

When I look at our team these days, I don't see a weak link. I love each and every one of them.

Klopp had once said, 'You want quality. You want to be brave. We want the fans to experience something special.'

He had given us all of that and more. Champions of England, Europe, and the world. That's our Mickey Mouse treble. It doesn't get any better than that.

Having led us from the darkness and ended our 30-year wait to be Champions Again, I think the last word should go to the man who delivered that victory to us.

As Klopp himself said, to describe his style of football, 'It's an emotional thing.'

It most certainly is.

The gap between titles was three decades too long. The journey was sometimes exhilarating and sometimes exhausting.

There were highs and lows, triumphs and disappointments, mistakes and missed opportunities.

Ultimately, there was success. And long may it last.

Through it all, the fans stayed loyal. We would have waited forever (although 30 years was quite long enough).

I guess that goes to show that we are true to our motto; we are with the team through thick and thin, the good times and the bad.

The victory parade may be on hold for now, but there's one thing that the team and the fans all know.

You'll never walk alone.

THE END

Other Books from the Publisher

In September 2017, amateur British football coach Justin Walley became the "National Team" Manager of Matabeleland, an obscure international team in western Zimbabwe.

Before him lay the seemingly impossible task of taking his group of unknown amateur footballers from an impoverished region of Africa to the "alternative world cup" – the CONIFA World Football Cup in London, the following summer. All that stood in his way was the small matter of no money, no resources, no salary, no visas, and no sponsors. There was one football, though... but no goal nets.

"Both a compelling personal journey and a lively, touching love letter to the pure spirit of football, packed with incident and never dull." **Stuart Maconie**, Radio DJ and popular culture critic.

"Matabeleland's struggle against fearsome odds to get to the 2018 CONIFA World Cup in London gets the fuller coverage it merits in a compelling diary from team coach Justin Walley." **When Saturday Comes**

"I recommend this; not your usual anodyne football book" **Brian Moore**, former World Rugby Player of the Year and England international, presenter and pundit.

"A cracking story and one that features the power of football and friendship on the journey. Walley tells it well ... he even persuades Liverpool legend Bruce Grobbelaar to become the Matabeleland goalkeeping coach at an M6 service station." **Late Tackle magazine**

OOH-AAH BOB BOOKAH… And so begins one of the most iconic chants in football. A chant for a cult hero who was renowned for his hard work, tenacity, honesty, and graciousness. A chant for a player who left everything on the pitch. It covers the challenges of dealing with fans' expectations, a long-term chronic injury that threatened to end his career, and how he dealt with the intrigue and machinations of football management.

Bob worked hard, gave his all, played wherever he was asked without complaint, wore every shirt (apart from the goalkeeper's), and was rewarded by playing or coaching in all four divisions of the Football League. Indeed, in a rollercoaster career that spanned almost five decades, Bob was a crucial part of teams – as either a player or coach – that celebrated six promotions and suffered three relegations. With contributions from former teammates, managers, and friends, the real Bob Booker is revealed in all his complexities. It is the kind, friendly, and humorous Bob that we all expected to find but also one who demonstrated grit, determination, courage, inner strength, guile and perseverance to forge such a long and successful career for himself.

"Brimming with entertaining anecdotes and revealing insight." **Henry Winter, Chief Football Writer, The Times**

"Confessor figure, comedian, coach, commissioned officer. Bob Booker may be classified as a number two, but he is one of football's hidden heroes. Greville Waterman shines a spotlight on him, and into the shadows of the game. Highly recommended." **Michael Calvin, Football Writer**

German Football has been on a roll in recent years: winners of the 2014 World Cup, Bundesliga club sides leading the way in Europe, a production line of superb talent coming through the system. Yet, twenty years ago – at Euro 2000 – it was all so different. Germany suffered one of their most humiliating tournament exits as dismal performances saw them finish bottom of their group with just one point… Immediately, the German FA set about fixing things. And rather than fudging matters, they introduced a raft of major changes designed to return German football to its sporting pinnacle in just 10 years.

In this entertaining, fascinating, and superbly-researched book, sportswriter Lee Price explores German football's 10–year plan. A plan that forced clubs to invest in youth, limit the number of foreign players in teams, build success without debt, and much more. The Bundesliga Blueprint details how German fans part-own and shape their clubs, how football is affordable, and the value of beer and a good sausage on match days. The book includes interviews from Michael Ballack, Jens Nowotny and Christoph Kramer, and the movers-and-shakers behind Germany's leading clubs including Schalke, Dortmund, and Paderborn. There is no doubt that German football is the envy of many nations. There is no doubt that, thanks to them, lessons should be learned by everyone else.

In 1988, 23-year-old American goalkeeper Justin Bryant thought a glorious career in professional football awaited him. He had just saved two penalties for his American club – the Orlando Lions – against Scotland's Dunfermline Athletic, to help claim the first piece of silverware in their history. He was young, strong, healthy, and confident. But professional football, he found, is rarely easy.

Small Time is the story of a life spent mostly in the backwaters of the game. As Justin negotiated the Non-League pitches of the Vauxhall-Opel League, and the many failed professional leagues of the U.S. in the 1980s and 90s, he struggled not only with his game, but his physical and mental health. Battling stress, social anxiety, a mysterious stomach ailment, and simple bad luck, he nonetheless experienced fleeting moments of triumph that no amount of money can buy. Football, he learned, is 95% blood, sweat, and tears; but if you love it enough, the other 5% makes up for it.

Planet Tennis. A world of high-profile tournaments, legendary competitors, up-and-coming youngsters, and fuzzy yellow balls. The Art of Tennis II is a brand-new collection of soulful and reflective tennis writing, providing 120 tennis narratives that deliver passionate insights, magical on-court moments, and a fresh perspective on the sport.

Starting at Wimbledon 2018, and following the women's and men's tours over the next 12 months, join Dominic J. Stevenson as he examines the rise and fall, resurrection, and departure of many of the competitors treading the boards of a truly global sport. Covering big names including Roger Federer, Serena Williams, Rafael Nadal, Naomi Osaka, Novak Djokovic, and Ashleigh Barty, the book also examines the games of many of tennis' young guns; names such as Alexander Zverev, Bianca Andreescu, Felix Auger-Aliassime, Belinda Bencic, and Stefanos Tsitsipas.

Lightning Source UK Ltd.
Milton Keynes UK
UKHW040411061120
372848UK00002BA/55